starting out:
the modern

NIGEL DAVIES

EVERYMAN CHESS

Gloucester Publishers plc   www.everymanchess.com

First published in 2008 by Gloucester Publishers plc (formerly Everyman Publishers plc), Northburgh House, 10 Northburgh Street, London EC1V 0AT

British Library Cataloguing-in-Publication Data
A catalogue record for this book is available from the British Library.

ISBN: 9781 85744 566 4

Distributed in North America by The Globe Pequot Press, P.O Box 480, 246 Goose Lane, Guilford, CT 06437-0480.

All other sales enquiries should be directed to Everyman Chess, Northburgh House, 10 Northburgh Street, London EC1V 0AT
tel: 020 7253 7887; fax: 020 7490 3708
email: info@everymanchess.com: website: www.everymanchess.com

Everyman is the registered trade mark of Random House Inc. and is used in this work under licence from Random House Inc.

EVERYMAN CHESS SERIES
Chief Advisor: Byron Jacobs
Commissioning editor: John Emms
Assistant editor: Richard Palliser

Typeset and edited by First Rank Publishing, Brighton.
Cover design by Horatio Monteverde.
Printed and bound in Great Britain by Clays, Bungay, Suffolk.

Contents

Dedicated to my late mother, Joan Davies

Bibliography

Megabase 2008

Informator

My formerly secret notebooks

Extensive use has also been made of several chess engines, notably *Hiarcs 9* and *Fritz 11*.

Introduction

What is the Modern Defence?

The Modern is a universal system of defence that can be played against any White opening. It is characterized by Black starting out with a fianchetto of his king's bishop with 1...g6 and 2...Bg7.

It differs from the Pirc Defence (1 e4 d6 2 d4 Nf6 3 Nc3 g6) in that Black delays developing his king's knight to f6. This knight may remain on g8 for some time or even come out to e7 or h6.

This book deals only with the Modern Defence, though Black can often transpose into a Pirc by playing ...Ng8-f6. I've pointed out the moments at which these Pirc transpositions may be a good idea, but the Pirc itself is not dealt with in this volume.

A Brief History of the Modern Defence

Although Louis Paulsen was playing 1...g6 in the 19th century, it wasn't until the 1950s that Ufimtsev, Robatsch and Kotov started to play the Modern with regularity at a high level. Gradually it attracted more adherents and by the 1960s 1...g6 could be found in the games of World Champions Botvinnik, Petrosian and Smyslov, plus a host of other strong Grandmasters.

In 1972 English GM Raymond Keene, together with George Botterill, wrote a seminal work on the Modern. This was to influence a generation of British players, of whom GMs David Norwood and Colin McNab proved to be the most enthusiastic practitioners.

Throughout the 1980s I played nothing but the Modern Defence as Black. In 1981 it helped me win an individual gold medal for my board in the World U26 Team Championships in Graz (in nine games I had eight Blacks, in which I conceded just two draws) and was also largely responsible for my first GM norm in Oslo in

1987. Later on I learned some more classical openings, but the Modern remains one of my major strike weapons when I need to win as Black.

Here is one of my key victories against the Norwegian IM Einar Gausel who would later rise to Grandmaster status:

Game 1
☐ E.Gausel ■ N.Davies
Oslo 1988

---

1 d4 d6 2 e4 g6 3 Nc3 Bg7 4 Bc4 Nc6 5 Be3

White should play 5 Nf3, after which 5...Nf6 transposes into a Pirc Defence.

5...Nf6 6 h3

Preventing 6...Ng4 but losing time for development.

6...e5 7 dxe5 Nxe5 8 Bb3 0-0 9 Qd2 b5! (Diagram 1)

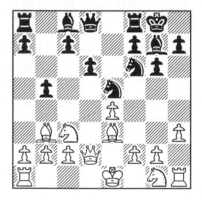
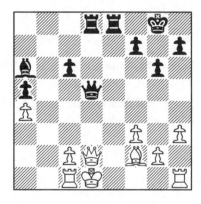

Diagram 1 (W)

Black seizes the initiative

Diagram 2 (W)

White is lost

White's neglect of development allows Black to take the initiative. If White captures the b5-pawn then e4 falls.

10 f3 b4 11 Nd5 Nxd5 12 Bxd5 c6 13 Bb3 a5 14 a4 d5

Blasting the centre open before White has got his king safe. If he had now tried to remedy this with 15 0-0-0 there would follow 15...Qf6, and after 16 Bd4 there is 16...c5!, distracting the bishop from the defence of b2.

15 exd5 Nc4! 16 Bxc4 Bxb2

Suddenly White is in desperate trouble; the threats include 17...Bxa1 and 17...Bc3, not to mention 17...Qh4+.

17 Ne2 Qh4+

Even stronger than capturing the rook on a1, as that will remain a threat.

18 Bf2 Qxc4 19 Rb1 Bc3 20 Nxc3 bxc3 21 Qd3 Re8+ 22 Kd1 Qa2 23 Rc1 Ba6 24 Qxc3 Qxd5+ 25 Qd2 Rad8 0-1 (Diagram 2)

The final position shows the true extent of White's misery.

What are the attractions of the Modern?

As I already said, the Modern is a universal system of defence that can be played against any White opening. It is characterized by its great flexibility with which it can adapt to any White set-up. It does not lead to clear and crisp positions, but to rather muddy and complex strategic and tactical problems.

It is this characteristic which makes it ideal for playing to win with Black: there are not the clean forcing lines and early resolution of tension which characterize the majority of openings. The delayed confrontation of pieces also makes it less vulnerable to sharp opening analysis – it requires understanding rather than memory.

How I play the Modern

My interpretation of the Modern Defence is to try to extend the range of Black's king's bishop by counterattacking against d4 with either ...c7-c5 or ...e7-e5. This is the sharpest and most interesting way to play the Modern. I do not like or particularly believe in the lines where Black tries to blockade with ...c7-c6 and ...d7-d5.

About this book

As part of the Everyman *Starting Out* series, this book is primarily aimed at players with little or no experience of the Modern Defence and who wish to get to grips with the plans and ideas. Each section begins with an introduction to the lines in question and an explanation of the strategy Black should adopt.

The illustrative games have been chosen for their instructive value and I have tried to explain the strategies for both sides. I've taken them from my own practice wherever possible, firstly because I understand them better and, secondly, because many of them were played against the kind of opposition that the reader may encounter.

Besides the games and explanations I've also included 30 test positions to help the reader get to grips with the sort of positions encountered in the Modern Defence. This sort of middlegame training is an excellent way of getting to understand the mechanics of different openings.

I've written this book mainly from Black's perspective as the vast majority of readers will be looking to play the Modern as Black. But it should also be useful to

White players, too, not least because they'll understand what their opponents are trying to do to them.

Wishing you luck with your future Modern Defence encounters.

Nigel Davies,
June 2008.

Chapter One

The Austrian Attack and Other f2-f4 Lines

Introduction

Illustrative Games

Introduction

The Austrian Attack with 4 f4 is one of White's sharpest attempts at refuting the Pirc and Modern Defences by assembling a battering ram of pawns in the centre. In this section I will look at both this and other lines in which White plays an early f2-f4. Personally speaking I like such positions as Black; pawns cannot move backwards and White is creating weaknesses in his position.

1 e4 g6 2 d4

Players who like to play 2 f4 against the Sicilian might also play it here. But in this situation 2 f4 is well met by 2...d5! **(Diagram 1)** as in Minev-Davies (Game 2).

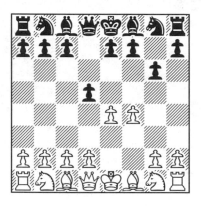

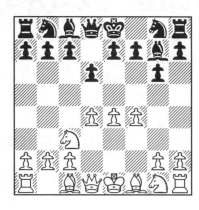

Diagram 1 (W)	Diagram 2 (B)
Exploding the centre	The Austrian Attack

Had White then played 3 exd5, Black could well consider offering a pawn with 3...Nf6!? 4 c4 c6 5 dxc6 Nxc6, with excellent play because of White's many weaknesses.

If White prevents ...d7-d5 by first playing 2 Nc3 and then meets 2...Bg7 with 3 f4, Black can if he likes transpose into the Vinken System of the Sicilian Defence with 3...c5, but in a game M.Hebden-N.Davies, South Wales 1984, I chose to give the game a different slant with 3...d6 4 Nf3 Bg4!?. After 5 h3 Bxf3 6 Qxf3 Nc6 7 Bb5 Qd7 8 Ne2 a6 9 Ba4 e6 10 c3 Nge7 the position was about equal.

2...Bg7 3 Nc3

White can also play 3 f4 in this position, a line known as the Three Pawns Attack. Compared to the Austrian Attack (with 3 Nc3 and 4 f4), White can reinforce his d4-pawn with c2-c3. Some books recommend that Black meets the Three Pawns Attack with 3...d5, starting to set up a blockade on the light squares. I don't like this approach and prefer to hit the d4-pawn with 3...d6 (or 3...c5 straight away) 4

Nf3 c5, for details of which see Jacobs-Davies (Game 3).

3...d6 4 f4 (Diagram 2)

The move that characterizes the Austrian Attack.

 NOTE: Although this may look a bit scary, White's advances expose his position.

4...e6!?

A move which requires some explanation. For many years I preferred 4...Nc6 in this position and after 5 Be3 would play 5...Nf6 6 Nf3 0-0 and then follow up with 7...e6!?, 8...Ne7, 9...b6 and 10...Bb7 to arrive at a very harmonious set-up. White's f4-f5 lever is restrained (thus restricting his dark-squared bishop behind the f4-pawn), Black pressurizes e4 and wants to counterattack White's centre with ...c7-c5. I was very successful with this plan which you can see in action in Engedal-Davies (Game 4).

Then one sad day (Vrnjacka Banja 1991), the Serbian GM Dragan Velimirovic played 5 Bb5! against me, which at the time was probably an innovation. After 5...a6 6 Bxc6 bxc6 7 Nf3 f5 8 e5 I found myself in a very passive position in which the g7-bishop wasn't working (see Game 5).

I was subsequently unable to find anything I particularly liked after 5 Bb5, but discovered that I could reach my favourite set-up via a different route. I would play first 4...e6 and then follow up with ...Ne7, ...Nd7, ...b7-b6, ...Bb7, ...0-0 and ...Nd7-f6! This idea was independently thought out by the Russian GM, Mikhail Krasenkow.

5 Nf3 Ne7 (Diagram 3)

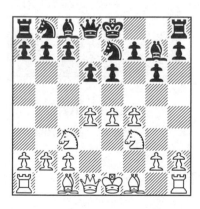

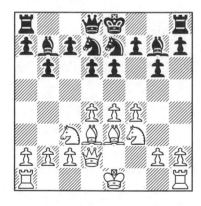

Diagram 3 (W)
Delaying counteraction

Diagram 4 (W)
A Hippopotamus formation

6 Bd3

My first game with 4...e6 was against the German player Baum in Gausdal 1993 (see Game 6). He chose 6 Be3 in this position and, following 6...Nd7 7 Qd2 a6, I only won after experiencing some awkward moments. I often go ...a7-a6 in this line to discourage White from castling long, but the drawback is that playing ...b7-b5 often makes it more difficult to lever White's centre with ...c7-c5. Instead, Krasenkow played 6...b6 7 Qd2 Bb7 8 Bd3 Nd7 **(Diagram 4)** 9 0-0-0 Nf6 in a couple of interesting games in the 1992/93 Hastings Challengers, Bryson-Krasenkow continuing 10 h3 0-0 11 Rhe1 c5 12 Bf2 c4!? 13 Bf1 b5 14 e5 Nh5 15 Nxb5 Bxf3 16 gxf3 d5 and White was in serious trouble (see Game 7).

I've also had 6 Be2 played against me, but things turned out well for Black in Baker-Davies (Game 8); and 6 Bc4 would transpose to Game 22 in Chapter Four.

6...Nd7 7 0-0 0-0 8 Ne2 c5 9 c3 Qb6!?

Staring at White's king along the b6-g1 diagonal.

10 Kh1 Nf6 11 Qe1 Bd7

An unusual development of the bishop in this line; Black wants to play ...Bb5.

12 Qh4 Rae8 13 e5 Nfd5 14 Ng5 h6 15 Ne4 Nf5 (Diagram 5)

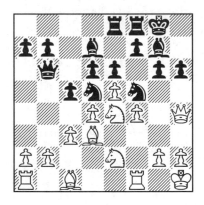

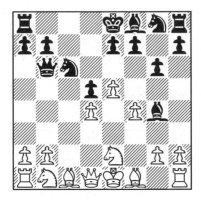

Diagram 5 (W)

Black has counterplay

Diagram 6 (W)

Building pressure against d4

and Black had counterplay in Knox-Davies (Game 9).

Illustrative Games

Game 2
□ **N.Minev** ■ **N.Davies**
Hamar 1983

---

1 e4 g6 2 f4 d5! 3 e5

The best move, trying to secure a space advantage. After 3 exd5 I like 3...Nf6, for example 4 c4 (if 4 Bb5+ Bd7 5 Bc4 Bg4 6 Nf3 Nxd5 recovers the pawn with the better game) 4...c6 (4...e6!? is another interesting gambit) 5 dxc6 Nxc6 gives Black good compensation for the pawn, largely thanks to White's weak pawn on f4. Play might continue 6 Nf3 Nd4 7 Nc3 Bg7 8 Nxd4 Qxd4 9 d3 Bf5 10 Qf3 0-0 11 Be2 Rfd8 with a good game for Black.

3...c5 4 c3 Nc6 5 d4

I think there's a case for delaying this move with 5 Na3, though I would still be very happy to play Black's position after 5...Nh6, for example.

5...cxd4 6 cxd4 Qb6 7 Ne2 Bg4 (Diagram 6)

TIP: Pinning a white knight on f3 or e2 like this can often help in Black's attack on d4.

8 Nbc3 e6 9 Be3 Nh6 10 Qd2 Nf5 11 0-0-0?

White's king proves to be very vulnerable over here. He should play 11 Bf2, which looks about equal after 11...h5.

11...Rc8 12 Bf2

After 12 h3 there might follow 12...Nxe3 13 Qxe3 Na5, when 14 b3 Nxb3+! 15 axb3 Bxe2 16 Bxe2 Qxb3 17 Rd3 Bb4 will recover the piece with interest.

12...Nb4 13 Kb1

This meets with a stunning reply which forces the win of White's queen. After either 13 a4 or 13 a3 Black can win the exchange with 13...Na2+, for example 14 Kb1 (or 14 Kc2 Nd6! threatening 15...Bf5+ and 15...Nc4) 14...Nxc3+ 15 Nxc3 Bxd1 etc.

13...Ne3! (Diagram 7) 14 Bxe3

After 14 Qxe3 Bf5+ 15 Kc1 Nxa2+ 16 Kd2 Qxb2+ 17 Ke1 Nxc3 Black wins back the piece having gained a couple of pawns into the bargain.

14...Bf5+ 15 Ka1 Nc2+ 16 Qxc2

Giving up the queen is White's best chance. After 16 Kb1 Nxe3+ 17 Ka1 Nc2+ 18 Kb1 Ba3 19 b3 Nxd4+ 20 Ka1 Nc2+ 21 Kb1 Ne3+ 22 Ka1 Nxd1 White would find himself the exchange and a pawn down.

16...Bxc2 17 Rc1 Bd3?!

A slip which gives White some counterplay. 17...Bf5 is simple and solid.

18 Nxd5! Rxc1+ 19 Nxc1 exd5 20 Bxd3 Bb4 21 f5 0-0 22 Ne2 Qa5 23 Rd1

23 Rc1 is less good because of 23...Bd2, when 24 Rc5 Qxc5 25 dxc5 Bxe3 leaves Black with a winning endgame.

23...Rc8 24 g4 Qa4 25 Rf1 Rc2 (Diagram 8)

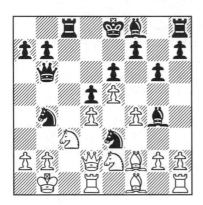
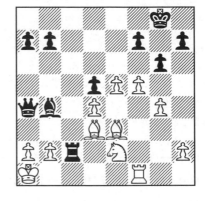

Diagram 7 (W)

Clearing f5 for the bishop

Diagram 8 (W)

Returning material to win

Giving the exchange back in order to get into White's position.

26 Bxc2 Qxc2 27 Nf4 Qe4 28 Bc1 Qxd4 29 e6 Qc4 30 exf7+ Kxf7 31 fxg6+ hxg6 32 Ne2+

32 Rd1 was better, though Black is still winning after 32...d4.

32...Ke8 33 Ng3 Qxg4 34 a3 Ba5 35 Be3 d4 36 Bf4 d3 37 Kb1 d2 0-1

Game 3
☐ **B.Jacobs** ■ **N.Davies**
Peterborough 1983

---

1 e4 g6 2 d4 Bg7 3 f4 d6

3...c5 is also good and would probably transpose after 4 d5 d6. In one of my games (Farley-Davies, 1984) my opponent defended his d-pawn with 4 c3, but after 4...cxd4 5 cxd4 Nc6!? 6 Nf3 d5 7 e5 Bg4 followed by ...Nh6 and ...Nf5, I developed tremendous pressure against d4.

4 Nf3

White can angle for a transposition into a Four Pawns Attack King's Indian with 4 c4 c5 5 d5. But Black is not obliged to cooperate and can instead play as Larsen did in S.Bouaziz-B.Larsen, Sousse Interzonal 1967. That game continued 5...e6 6 Nc3 exd5 7 cxd5 Ne7!? (a noteworthy development of the knight, which can be combined with ...f7-f5) 8 Nf3 0-0 9 Be2 Bg4 10 0-0 Nd7 11 Kh1 a6 12 a4 Qc7 13 Be3 Rae8! 14 h3 Bxf3 15 Bxf3 Nf5! 16 Bf2 Nd4 17 Bxd4 cxd4 18 Ne2 Qb6 and Black already had the initiative.

4...c5 (Diagram 9)

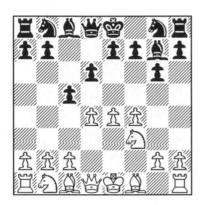

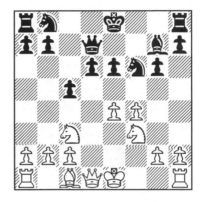

Diagram 9 (W)

Undermining the centre

Diagram 10 (W)

Black has a central pawn majority

 WARNING: In the Modern you must always be thinking about how to undermine White's centre. Letting it sit there for too long can have dangerous consequences!

5 d5

After 5 c3 I've had good results with the move 5...Qa5!?, threatening to whittle away White's central pawns with ...c5xd4 (White can't recapture with the c3-pawn). For example, 6 Nbd2 cxd4 7 Nb3 (7 Nc4 Qd8 8 cxd4 d5 9 exd5 Nf6 left White's position full of holes in Jung-Davies, Peterborough Open 1986) 7...Qb6 8 Nbxd4 (8 cxd4 Bg4 9 Be2 Nc6 is very awkward for White) 8...Nc6 9 Bb5 Nf6 10 Qd3 0-0 11 Be3 Qc7 12 h3 Bd7 13 g4 Nxd4 14 Nxd4 e5! and White's exposed position started to fall apart in Summers-Davies, Cardiff 1996.

5...Nf6 6 Bb5+

White's most natural move is 6 Nc3, though Black is doing fine after 6...0-0 7 Be2 e6. V.Zurakhov-V.Korchnoi, USSR Championship, Leningrad 1956, continued 8 0-0 exd5 9 exd5 Na6 10 Ng5 Nc7 11 a4 h6 12 Nf3 Re8 13 Bc4 Bf5 14 h3 Ne4 15 Nxe4 Bxe4 and Black had the better game.

6...Bd7 7 Bxd7+ Qxd7

I didn't like 7...Nbxd7 because of 8 e5 dxe5 9 fxe5 Ng4 10 e6 fxe6 11 Ng5, though Black might try some other moves on the way.

8 Nc3 e6 9 dxe6 fxe6 (Diagram 10)

Capturing this way gives Black a central pawn majority

10 Qe2 0-0 11 e5 Nd5 12 Ne4 dxe5 13 fxe5 Qc6

Perhaps I should have opted for the more natural 13...Nc6, when 14 Nxc5 Qc8!? 15 0-0 Nxe5 is very good for Black.

14 c4 Nf4 15 Bxf4 Rxf4 16 Nc3 Qa6 17 0-0 Qxc4 18 Qe3 Nc6 (Diagram 11)

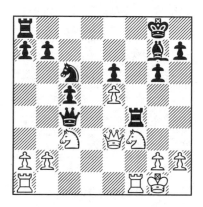

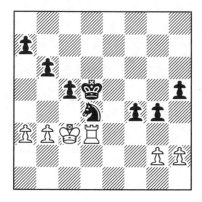

Diagram 11 (W)

Black plans an exchange sacrifice

Diagram 12 (W)

Forward patrol!

Hitting the pawn on e5 whilst preparing the following exchange sacrifice.

19 b3 Qb4 20 a3 Rxf3 21 Rxf3

21 axb4?? Rxe3 leaves White a piece down.

21...Qd4 22 Rd1 Bxe5 23 Qxd4

23 Rxd4? Bxd4 wins the queen back and leaves Black two pawns up.

23...Bxd4+ 24 Kh1 Rf8 25 Ne4 Rf5 26 Rxf5 exf5 27 Nd6 b6 28 Nb5 Kf7 29 Nxd4 Nxd4

Rooks are usually very good against knights in the endgame, but here Black's active king tips the balance in his favour.

30 Rd3 Ke6 31 Kg1 Kd5 32 Kf2 f4 33 Ke1 h5 34 Kd2

34 h4 Ke4 35 Rc3 Nf5 hits the newly weakened h4-pawn.

34...g5 35 Kc3 g4 (Diagram 12) 36 b4?!

36 Rd1 would have been more tenacious.

36...Ke4 37 bxc5 bxc5 38 Kd2 c4 39 Rc3 Nb3+ 40 Ke2 Kd4 41 Rc2 c3 42 h3 Kc4 43 Kd1 Kd3 44 hxg4 hxg4 45 Rf2 Nd4 0-1

The threat of 46...c2+ is a killer.

Game 4
□ **K.Engedal** ■ **N.Davies**
Gausdal 1990

---

1 e4 g6 2 d4 Bg7 3 Nc3 d6 4 f4 Nc6

I was later to abandon this move after Dragan Velimirovic responded with 5 Bb5 in 1991 (see the next game). Since then I have answered the Austrian Attack (4 f4) with 4...e6 followed by ...Ne7, ...Nd7, ...b7-b6 and ...Bb7, obtaining a similar set-up to the game.

5 Be3 Nf6 6 Nf3 e6 7 Be2 0-0 8 0-0 Ne7 9 Nd2 b6 10 a4 a6 11 Qe1 c5 (Diagram 13)

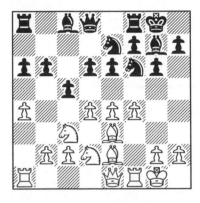
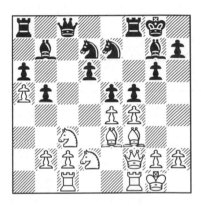

Diagram 13 (W)	**Diagram 14 (W)**
Black finally strikes back	And now on the kingside

Black's usual way of challenging White's set-up from this structure. Here it proves especially effective because White has played the rather artificial 9 Nd2.

12 Qf2 Bb7 13 Bf3 Qc7 14 a5 cxd4

Reaching a kind of Sicilian Defence structure.

15 Bxd4 b5 16 Bb6 Qc8 17 Rac1 Nd7 18 Bd4

18 Be3 was better, as now Black rips apart what is left of White's centre.

18...e5

NOTE: This is a typical counterattacking move in both the Sicilian and the Modern.

19 Be3 f5! (Diagram 14)

The opening of the position proves good for Black as his pieces are better placed. Note that White's king also proves weak, a consequence of 4 f4!

20 g3 exf4 21 gxf4 b4 22 Nd1 Nf6 23 Qg2 fxe4 24 Nxe4 Nxe4 25 Bxe4 Bxe4 26 Qxe4 Qg4+ 27 Kh1

27 Qg2 Qf5 would also have been unpleasant for White.

27...Nf5 28 Qxb4

A suicidal snatch, but it is already rather difficult to give White good advice.

28...Ng3+ 29 Kg1

Taking the knight allows 29...Qh3+ followed by 30...Qxg3+ and 31...Rf5.

29...Nxf1+ 30 Kxf1 Qf3+ 31 Kg1 Rae8 32 Qd2 Rxf4 0-1

White has had enough. 33 Bxf4 is answered by 33...Re2 threatening both mate and the queen.

Game 5
☐ **D.Velimirovic** ■ **N.Davies**
Vrnjacka Banja 1991

---

1 e4 d6 2 d4 g6 3 Nc3 Bg7 4 f4 Nc6 5 Bb5!? (Diagram 15)

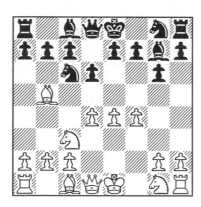
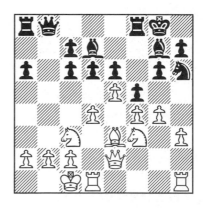

Diagram 15 (B)	Diagram 16 (B)
An important idea	White begins the assault

An unpleasant move for Black. In the game I find it difficult to get counterplay and ultimately get poleaxed on the kingside.

TIP: By playing 4...e6 instead Black can avoid this pin.

5...a6 6 Bxc6+ bxc6 7 Nf3 f5?!

This leaves the Modern bishop on g7 very passive. I think that 7...Bg4 is a better try, though there too I prefer White. For example, 8 0-0 Qb8 9 h3 Bxf3 10 Rxf3 Qb6 11 Be3!? Qxb2 12 Bf2 Qb7 13 f5 c5 14 Rb1 Qc6 15 Nd5 Nf6 16 c4 gave White a very strong initiative in E.Lobron-Z.Azmaiparashvili, Groningen 1993.

8 e5 Nh6 9 Qe2 e6 10 Be3 0-0 11 0-0-0 Bd7 12 h3 Qb8 13 g4 (Diagram 16)

Velimirovic is never backward at coming forward.

13...Qb4

After 13...fxg4 14 hxg4 Nxg4 there would follow 15 Rxh7 Kxh7 16 Ng5+ Kg8 17 Qxg4 with a winning attack.

14 a3 Qb7 15 g5 Nf7 16 h4 Rfb8 17 b3 c5 18 h5 cxd4 19 hxg6 hxg6 20 Nxd4 (Diagram 17)

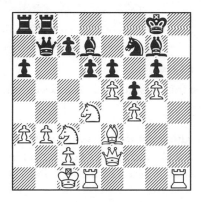

Diagram 17 (B)

Coming down the h-file

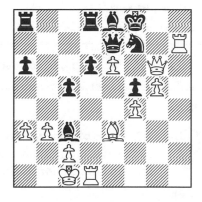

Diagram 18 (W)

Black goes down in flames

20...c5

On 20...dxe5 White can play 21 fxe5 (or maybe even 21 Qh2, for example 21...exd4 22 Qh7+ Kf8 23 Qxg6 Nxg5 24 Bxd4 Bxd4 25 Qxg5 with too many threats) 21...Nxe5 22 Bf4 Nf7 23 Qh2 e5 24 Qh7+ Kf8 25 Rh6 Bxh6 26 gxh6 and now 26...exf4 27 Re1 leaves Black defenceless against the threat of 28 Qg7 mate.

21 Nxf5 exf5 22 Qh2 Bc6 23 Qh7+ Kf8 24 Rh2 Qe7

After 24...Bf3 25 Qxg6 Bxd1 26 Nxd1 Black would be faced with the threat of 27 Rh7.

25 Qxg6 Rd8?

After this I go down in flames. I could have kept the game out of the magazines with 25...Nxe5 26 fxe5 Qxe5 27 Qxd6+ Qxd6 28 Rxd6 Be5, though admittedly the endgame is probably lost after 29 Rxc6 Bxh2 30 Rxc5 f4 31 Rf5+ Kg7 32 Bxf4 Bxf4+ 33 Rxf4.

26 e6

26 Nd5 was also very strong.

26...Bxc3?

26...Re8 was the best shot, but still good for White after 27 Rh7 Nh8 28 Rxh8+ Bxh8 29 Rxd6! etc.

27 Rh7 Be8 (Diagram 18) 28 Rdh1

28 Rd4! would have been even more spectacular.

28...Ra7 29 Bd2 Bd4 30 c3 Nh6 31 Qxh6+ 1-0

Game 6
☐ **B.Baum** ■ **N.Davies**
Gausdal 1993

---

1 e4 d6 2 d4 g6 3 Nc3 Bg7 4 f4 e6 5 Nf3 Ne7 6 Be3 Nd7

Krasenkow has shown a preference for 6...b6 in this position (see the next game).

7 Qd2 a6

TIP: This is often a good move if you think White wants to castle queenside. But it is not clear that Black should always go ...b7-b5 in this type of position as the ...c7-c5 break is aided by a pawn on b6!

8 Bd3 b5

I think that 8...c5 might be better here, for example 9 0-0 0-0 10 Qf2 cxd4 11 Bxd4 e5 12 fxe5 Nc6 13 exd6 Nxd4 14 Nxd4 Ne5 15 Be2 Qxd6 with compensation for the pawn.

9 0-0 Nf6 10 Rae1 Ng4 (Diagram 19)

After 10...Bb7 there is 11 Bf2 when White's centre is well supported. I didn't especially like the text move, but Black must obtain some compensation for his lack of breathing space.

11 f5 Nxe3 12 Qxe3 0-0 13 g4 b4

Black is in serious danger of being suffocated – something has to be done in the centre.

14 Nd1 exf5 15 gxf5 d5 16 Qf4! (Diagram 20) 16...f6

Not a pleasant move to play, but it's difficult to find a decent alternative. 16...gxf5

17 exf5 would give White easy play; and 16...dxe4 17 Bxe4 Nd5 18 Bxd5 Qxd5 19 f6 is simply horrible.

17 Ne3 c6 18 c3?!

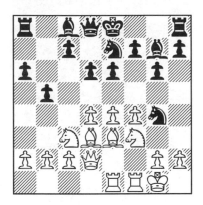

Diagram 19 (W)

Eliminating the dark-squared bishop

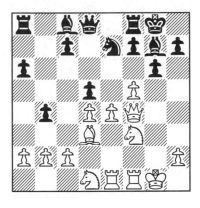

Diagram 20 (B)

How should Black defend?

Supporting the centre like this looks good, but in reality the weakness of c3 is more serious than the shadow of counterplay against the d4-pawn. After 18 Kh1, for example, Black would be left in an unenviable position.

18...bxc3 19 bxc3 Kh8 20 Kh1 Ra7 21 Rg1 Qa5!

A counterattack, not only against c3 but also the hidden target on f5. Thus 22 Rc1 is met by 22...dxe4 followed by 23...gxf5 etc..

22 exd5 Qxc3 23 Bb1 g5! (Diagram 21) 24 Qg4 Rb7

During the game I felt very proud of this idea, which cold-bloodedly allows the d-pawn to advance to d6. But in the cold light of day I can no longer see any serious objection to simply 24...Nxd5 25 Nxd5 cxd5.

25 d6 Ng8 26 Qe4

The threat was 26...Rxb1.

26...Bd7 27 Rc1 Qb4 28 d5

I later saw my opponent analysing this position with Rashkovsky. He tried to improve with 28 Nc4, and after 28...Re8 they were very enthusiastic about 29 Nce5!. But 28...Nh6 is a safer move.

28...Qxd6 29 dxc6 Rxb1 30 Qxb1

Perhaps 30 cxd7 was a better try, but even so I prefer Black's chances. Despite White's temporarily more active pieces his king is not very safe. And a pawn is a pawn.

30...Bxc6 31 Rgf1 Ba8 32 Kg1 Rb8 33 Qc2 Rb4 34 Nc4? (Diagram 22)

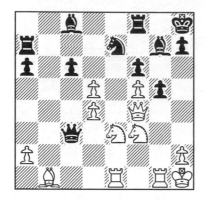
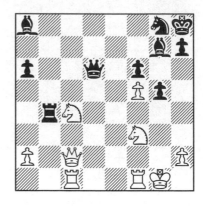

Diagram 21 (W)

The kingside must be closed

Diagram 22 (B)

Leading to the abyss

This leads to the abyss as White's weakened king position needs the protection of this knight. In mitigation it might be claimed that it is especially difficult to play such positions when short of time.

34...Qf4 35 a3?

35 Ncd2 g4 is not a pleasant alternative, but the text is essentially equivalent to resignation.

35...Qg4+ 36 Qg2 Rxc4 37 Qxg4 Rxg4+ 38 Kf2 Rf4 39 Ke2 Re4+ 40 Kd3 Ra4 41 Rc3 Be4+ 42 Ke3

After 42 Kd2 there is 42...g4; and after 42 Ke2 simply 42...Bxf5 is hopeless for White (if 43 Nxg5 fxg5 hits the rook on c3).

42...Ne7 0-1

White, having sealed 43 Ke2 in this hopeless situation, failed to turn up for the resumption.

Game 7
□ **D.Bryson** ■ **M.Krasenkow**
Hastings 1992/93

---

1 e4 g6 2 d4 Bg7 3 Nc3 d6 4 f4 e6!? 5 Nf3 Ne7 6 Be3 b6 7 Qd2 Bb7 8 0-0-0 Nd7 9 Bd3 (Diagram 23)

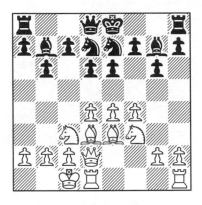

Diagram 23 (B)

Time to decide on a plan

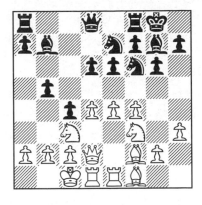

Diagram 24 (W)

A thematic pawn sacrifice

9 Qe1 a6 10 Bd3 was a resounding success for White in V.Kotronias-J.Hebert, Montreal 2002: 10...c5 11 Rf1 0-0?! 12 g4 Nf6 13 Qh4 cxd4 14 Nxd4 Nd7 15 f5 exf5 16 exf5 Nc6 17 Bg5 Bf6 18 Ne4 1-0. Instead, Finkel suggests 10...b5!? 11 g4 Nb6 12 Rf1 Qd7 13 h4 0-0-0 "with a slightly passive, but very flexible position."

9...Nf6

Black has an interesting alternative in 9...d5, for example 10 exd5 (10 e5 c5 isn't clear either) 10...Nxd5 11 Nxd5 Bxd5 12 Ne5 0-0 13 c4 Bb7 14 h4 h5 15 Qc2 Nf6 16 Rhg1 Ng4 17 Nxg4 hxg4 18 h5 Bxd4 19 Bxd4 Qxd4 20 hxg6 Qxf4+ 21 Kb1 f5 22 c5 was R.Castro Santimoteo-I.Efimov, Olot 1993, and now 22...Bd5 was probably best when White is struggling to justify his aggressive play.

One other possibility is 9...a6, for example 10 h4 c5 11 h5 Qc7 12 dxc5 (12 h6 Bf8 would leave White with nothing to play for on the kingside) 12...bxc5 13 hxg6 hxg6 14 Rxh8+ Bxh8 15 f5 gxf5 16 exf5 exf5 17 Bf4 0-0-0 18 Qe2 Nb6 19 Bxa6 Bxc3 20 bxc3 Ned5 and Black had excellent play in M.Solleveld-J.Hickl, German League 2002.

10 h3

10 f5 exf5 11 exf5 Qd7 12 Bh6 Bxh6 13 Qxh6 0-0-0 14 Rhf1 Rde8! 15 a3 Ned5 16 Nxd5 Bxd5! 17 Rde1 Rxe1+ 18 Rxe1 Re8 was equal in E.Mortensen-M.Krasenkow from the same tournament.

10...0-0 11 Rhe1

Black also gets counterplay after other moves, for example 11 g4 c5 (11...d5 12 e5 Ne4 and 11...b5 12 g5 b4 13 gxf6 bxc3 14 Qxc3 Bxf6 also seem playable) 12 dxc5 bxc5 13 g5 Nh5 intending ...Qb6 and ...Rfb8; or if 11 Bf2 b5!? (or 11...c5) 12 e5 b4 etc.

11...c5

Another option is 11...b5!?, for example 12 Bxb5 (or 12 e5 b4) 12...Nxe4 13 Nxe4 Bxe4 14 Ng5 Bd5 (14...Qb8 also seems quite playable) 15 c4 a6!? 16 cxd5 axb5 17 dxe6 f6 18 Nf7 Qc8 19 d5 Rxa2 with a very strong attack.

12 Bf2

White is more or less ready to play e4-e5, but Black is prepared.

12...c4!? 13 Bf1?!

If 13 Bxc4 Nxe4 14 Nxe4 Bxe4 15 Rxe4 d5 16 Bxd5 Qxd5 forks the rook on e4 and pawn on a2.

13...b5! (Diagram 24)

> TIP: With White's king castled on the queenside Black can often offer the b-pawn as bait. If White takes it he opens the b-file against his own king.

14 e5 Nh5!

Making it a 'real' pawn sacrifice.

Black had another possibility in 14...b4, but White can then play 15 Nb5 (15 exf6 bxc3 16 Qxc3 Bxf6 17 Bxc4 Rc8 is nice for Black) 15...Ne4 16 Rxe4 Bxe4 17 Nxd6 with compensation for the exchange. For example 17...c3 18 bxc3 bxc3 19 Qxc3 Nd5 20 Qa3 Bxf3 21 Qxf3 Qa5 22 Rd3 Qxa2?? 23 Ra3 wins Black's queen.

15 Nxb5?!

The critical line is 15 exd6, after which 15...Nf5 (15...Nd5 is also worth considering) 16 Nxb5 (16 Ne5 is answered by 16...Nxf4! because 17 Qxf4? Bh6 wins the queen) 16...Nxf4 17 Kb1 Nxh3 (17...Bh6 is also interesting) 18 Be3 leads to a very complex position.

15...Bxf3! 16 gxf3 d5 (Diagram 25)

After this the position is clearly better for Black: White can do nothing on the kingside, whilst Black's prospects on the other flank are just excellent.

17 Nd6 Bh6 18 Be3 Qb6 19 h4

Or 19 c3 Rab8.

19...Nf5

19...Rab8 20 c3 Nc8 was a good alternative.

20 Nxf5 exf5 21 Re2 Rfb8 22 Qc3?

Perhaps this is already the decisive mistake as now White seems unable to stop the attack along the b-file. 22 c3 looks best, intending a mass defence of the b2-pawn.

22...Bf8 23 a3 Rb7 24 Kb1

Heading for the hills with 24 Kd2 leads to a bad endgame for White after

24...Qxb2 25 Qxb2 Rxb2 etc.

24...Qa6 (Diagram 26) 25 Rg2?!

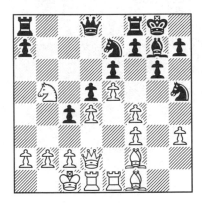

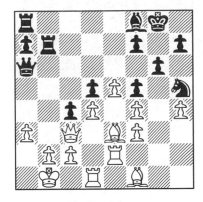

Diagram 25 (W)

Black is clearly better

Diagram 26 (W)

Black has a ferocious attack

If 25 Ka2? Bb4 wins the queen. 25 Bc1 is probably more tenacious, but in any case Black has a ferocious attack after 25...Bxa3.

25...Bxa3 26 b3

Black can meet 26 Bc1 with 26...Nxf4! when 27 Bxf4 (27 Rg3 Rab8 is hopeless for White) 27...Rxb2+ 28 Qxb2 Bxb2 29 Kxb2 Rb8+ 30 Kc1 Qa1+ 31 Kd2 Qxd4+ picks up the bishop on f4

26...Rab8 27 Qa1

Or 27 Bc1 Qa4 28 Bxa3 Rxb3+ 29 cxb3 Rxb3+ 30 Rb2 Rxa3 etc.

27...Qa4 28 Qa2

After 28 Rdd2, one way for Black to win is via 28...Ng3!, for example 29 Bxc4 (29 Rxg3 Rxb3+ 30 cxb3 Qxb3+ is carnage) 29...dxc4 30 d5 cxb3 etc.

28...cxb3 29 cxb3 Rxb3+ 30 Ka1 Rxe3 31 Rc2 Bb2+! 32 Kb1 Ra3 0-1

This wins, and in fact White resigned. But Black could also have forced mate with 32...Qxa2+ 33 Kxa2 Ra3+ 34 Kb1 Ra1 mate.

Game 8
☐ **C.Baker** ■ **N.Davies**
Crewe 1996

1 e4 g6 2 d4 Bg7 3 Nc3 d6 4 f4 e6!? 5 Nf3 Ne7 6 Be2 Nd7 7 0-0 b6 8 Qe1?! (Diagram 27)

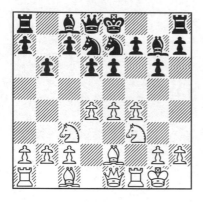

Diagram 27 (B)

Playing for mate!

Diagram 28 (W)

Making ready to defend h7

Actually this is the start of a overly brutal plan. I answer this flank attack with the classic recipe, a counterblow in the centre.

8...Bb7 9 Kh1 0-0 10 Qh4?!

White should try to prevent the coming ...c7-c5 lever with 10 Be3 intending 11 Rd1. Now Black hits back.

10...c5 11 Be3 Nf6!

Suddenly the centre is collapsing, as 12 e5 can be met by 12...Nf5 and 12 Bd3 by 12...c4!. Rather than go for a miserable defence White gamely sacrifices two pawns for piece activity, but in the face of accurate defence it can never be enough.

12 Rad1 Bxe4! 13 Nxe4 Nxe4 14 f5 gxf5!

Assuring central control by capturing towards the centre. In this particular position this is more important than the integrity of the kingside pawn shield.

15 dxc5 bxc5 16 Ng5 Nxg5 17 Bxg5 f6 18 Be3 Rc8!

Not only defending against the threat of 19 Bxc5, but also preparing to eject a white bishop from d3 with the push ...c5-c4.

19 Rf3 Ng6 20 Qh5 Rf7! (Diagram 28)

Preparing for lateral defence of h7.

21 Rh3 Bf8 22 Rg1 c4 23 g4 f4 24 Bd4 e5 25 Bc3 Qe8!

The last precise move, after which Black's central pawn mass starts to roll forwards. It was not too late to mess things up: 25...d5 26 g5 f5? could have been met by 27 Bxe5!! Nxe5 28 g6 Rg7 29 Qxh7+!! etc.

26 g5 f5 27 Bf3 Qe6

And not 27...e4?? 28 Qxg6+.

28 Re1 Rd7

Finally putting an end to any mating combinations based on Qxg6. Now it's all over.

29 Kg1 d5 30 Kh1 e4 31 Bg2 Qf7 32 Bf6 f3 33 Bxf3 exf3 34 Qxf3 d4 35 Qxf5 Qd5+ 36 Qxd5+ Rxd5 37 Rd1 Bg7 38 Rf3 Bxf6 39 gxf6 Kf7 40 b3 cxb3 41 cxb3 Rc6 42 Rh3 h5 43 Rhd3 Rcd6 0-1

Game 9
☐ **V.Knox** ◼ **N.Davies**
Manchester 1999

"In this characteristically provocative game, Nigel Davies wound up Vic Knox, a fine old slugger with a huge punch when it connects, beyond the point of bearing. Knox lashed out between moves 12 and 15, but after 15 ...Nf5! and even more tellingly 17 ...Nb4 and 18 ...Bb5, it all rebounded in his face. Insufferable cheek!" – Jon Speelman in *The Independent*.

1 e4 g6 2 d4 Bg7 3 Nc3 d6 4 f4 e6 5 Nf3 Ne7 6 Bd3

This looks like White's most natural developing move.

6...Nd7 7 0-0 0-0 8 Ne2 c5 9 c3 Qb6 10 Kh1 (Diagram 29)

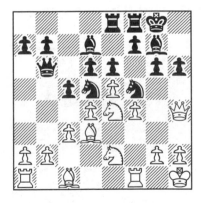

Diagram 29 (B)

How should Black continue?

Diagram 30 (W)

A key defensive move

10...Nf6

10...f5 was later played in M.Preuss-J.Sapienza, Moron 2004, though I don't like Black's king's bishop after 11 e5. Of course Sapienza wouldn't have known about this game against Knox from a weekend tournament, but blockading moves such as ...f7-f5 are just not in the spirit of this opening.

11 Qe1 Bd7 12 Qh4 Rae8 13 e5 Nfd5 14 Ng5 h6 15 Ne4 Nf5! (Diagram 30) 16 Qf2?!

White could and should have played 16 dxc5, after which 16...dxc5 (16...Nxh4? 17 cxb6 dxc5 18 bxa7 is good for White) 17 Qh3 Rd8 is probably about equal.

Now Black takes the initiative:

16...cxd4 17 cxd4?!

Perhaps it was better to play 17 Nxd4, though after 17...dxe5 18 fxe5 Bxe5 19 Nxf5 exf5 20 Nc5 Bc6 21 Bxh6 Nf4 22 Bxf4 Bxf4 23 Qxf4 Qxc5 I still prefer Black because of the strong bishop on c6 bearing down on g2.

17...Nb4 18 Bb1 Bb5 19 Nf6+?

This deprives my kingside of the dark-squared bishop, but there's a high price to pay: the rest of Black's pieces find very good squares. 19 N4c3 was better, though still good for Black after 19...Nd3.

19...Bxf6 20 exf6 Rc8 21 g4?

Hiarcs 9 feels it's necessary to play 21 Bxf5, though after 21...exf5 Black's control of the light squares leaves him well on top.

21...Qc6+

There is a good alternative in 21...Nxd4 22 Nxd4 Bxf1 23 Be3 Nd5, but I was looking for a way which denied White of any counterplay.

22 Kg1 Bxe2 23 Qxe2 Nxd4 (Diagram 31)

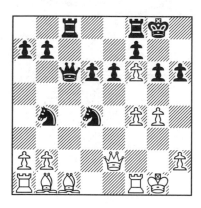

Diagram 31 (W)

Another important pawn falls

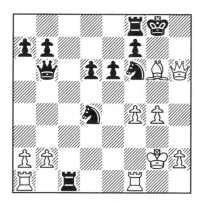

Diagram 32 (B)

The final throw

24 Qe3

Trying desperately to get the queen to h6. After 24 Qe4 Qxe4 25 Bxe4 d5 26 Bg2 Ne2+ 27 Kh1 Nxc1 28 Raxc1 Nd3 29 Rxc8 Rxc8 White would have a lost endgame.

24...Qb6

Or 24...Qc5!? 25 Be4 d5 26 a3 dxe4 27 axb4 Qd5 with a decisive advantage.

25 Kg2 Nd5 26 Qh3?

26 Qf2 is mandatory, though Black can then win with 26...Nxf6 27 Be3 Rc4 etc.

26...Rxc1! 27 Qxh6

If 27 Rxc1 Nxf4+ and White loses his queen.

27...Nxf6 28 Bxg6 (Diagram 32)

Desperation.

28...Qxb2+ 29 Rf2 Qxf2+! 0-1

After 30 Kxf2 Nxg4+, Black regains the queen with interest.

Summary

White's aggressive f2-f4 plans are dangerous for both sides. Against the Austrian Black can inhibit any further advances with 4...e6 followed by ...Ne7, and then prepare a central counterattack ...c7-c5. In the complex positions that follow it is often White's king that comes under pressure through lack of decent pawn cover.

Chapter Two

Bg5 Systems

Introduction

Illustrative Games

Introduction

In my opinion the Byrne System with 3 Nc3 and 4 Bg5 is one of the most dangerous at White's disposal, yet it tends to crop up surprisingly little in practice. Once again I will show you my own method of dealing with it based on the counterattacking move 4...Nc6.

1 e4 g6 2 d4 Bg7 3 Nc3

The immediate 3 Bg5 runs into 3...c5 4 c3 cxd4 5 cxd4 Qb6, so White must first prepare it.

3...d6 4 Bg5 (Diagram 1)

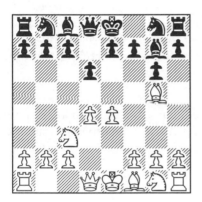

Diagram 1 (B)	Diagram 2 (W)
The Byrne System	Black plans ...Nh6-f7

One other move for White deserves a mention and that is 4 Bf4. The Hungarian IM Tamas Horvath played this against me in Copenhagen in 1984. I replied with my usual formula of 4...Nc6 and the game continued 5 Bb5 a6 6 Bxc6+ bxc6 7 Qd2 Rb8 8 0-0-0 Bd7 9 Nge2 Qc8 10 f3 Qb7 11 b3 Qb4 12 Kb1 a5 13 g4 a4 14 h4 h5 with a double-edged position. Very similar play to this can arise after 4 Bg5 Nc6 5 Bb5, should White choose to castle long.

4...Nc6

Counterattacking d4, my favourite strategy!

5 Bb5

One of several ways to defend d4, while White can also hit the knight on c6 with the move 5 d5.

a) 5 Nf3 was played in Soltis-Adorjan, Birmingham 1973 (see Game 11).

b) 5 Nge2 gave me some problems against Mark Tseitlin in the 1994 Beersheva tournament. In that game I played 5...Nf6 6 Qd2 (6 d5 Ne5 7 Nd4 c5 8 Bb5+ Bd7 9 Bxd7+ Qxd7 10 Nf3 reaches Test Position 5, in which you are invited to find Black's next move) 6...h6 7 Bh4 g5 8 Bg3 Nh5, but after 9 Nd5 e6 10 Ne3 Nxg3 11 hxg3 Qf6 12 c3 h5 13 f3 Bd7 14 g4 hxg4 15 Nxg4 Qg6 16 Rxh8+ Bxh8 17 Ng3 0-0-0 18 Bd3 White had built up some strong pressure and I had to defend the position very carefully.

I think that Black has an interesting alternative to this in 5...f6!? 6 Be3 e5 **(Diagram 2)** intending to develop further with ...Nh6-f7, castle kingside, and eventually play ...f6-f5. See Yermolinsky-Azmaiparashvili (Game 10) for an example of this treatment.

c) On 5 d5 Black may well be able to play the sharp 5...Nd4. In practice I have used 5...Ne5, after which 6 f4 Nd7 7 Nf3 c6 8 Qd2 cxd5 9 exd5 Ngf6 10 0-0-0 Nc5 11 Nd4 was the continuation of my game against Artashes Minasian in the 1990 Lyons Open. In this position I should have played the move 11...Bd7 followed by 12...Rc8, when Black has got counterplay on the c-file without having committed his king.

5...a6 6 Bxc6+ bxc6 7 Nge2

Probably the most harmonious way to develop. I had 7 Qd2 played against me by a Mr. Lagunes in Val Thorens 1984. After 7...Rb8 White even offered to sacrifice his b-pawn with 8 h4?!, but following 8...h6 9 Be3 Rxb2 he found himself without any compensation.

7...Rb8 8 Rb1 Nf6 (Diagram 3)

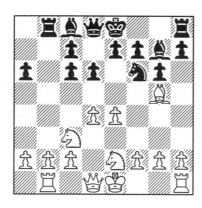

Diagram 3 (W)

e4-e5 is no longer a problem

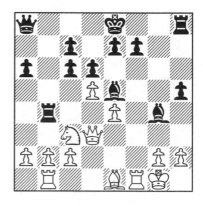

Diagram 4 (W)

18...Qa8! deserves a diagram!

Developing the knight when e4-e5 is no longer a problem.

9 0-0 h6 10 Bh4

Knowing the sharp uncompromising style of Jonathan Mestel he probably wanted Black to play 10...g5. But in my opinion it would have been wiser for White to maintain this bishop with, say, 10 Bf4.

10...g5! 11 Bg3 Nh5 12 f4 Rb4

A very imaginative move, putting pressure on the centre from a quite unexpected direction. White may have been wiser to choose 12 f3 rather than 12 f4, but this was not the decisive mistake.

13 Be1 Bg4! 14 Qd3 Nxf4 15 Nxf4 gxf4 16 Rxf4 h5 17 d5 Be5 18 Rf1 Qa8! (Diagram 4)

Black's original manoeuvres make this game a favourite of mine. We are following Mestel-Botterill, British Championship 1974, in which Black went on to score a famous victory (see Game 12).

Illustrative Games

Game 10
□ **A.Yermolinsky** ■ **Z.Azmaiparashvili**
Groningen 1993

1 d4 d6 2 e4 g6 3 Nc3 Bg7 4 Bg5 Nc6 5 Nge2 f6!?

I've usually played 5...Nf6 in this position, but I like Azmaiparashvili's move rather more. Black gets to strongpoint his e5-pawn and can develop his king's knight to h6 and f7.

6 Be3 e5 7 Qd2 Nge7 8 d5 Nb8 9 0-0-0 0-0?! (Diagram 5)

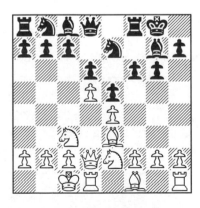

Diagram 5 (W)

Castling into the attack

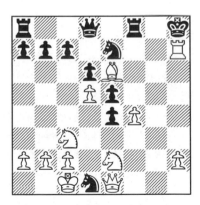

Diagram 6 (B)

A rook sacrifice!

In my view this move is premature here. Black should be careful about committing his king in the Modern. After the game Azmaiparashvili felt he might have done better with the immediate 9...Nd7 10 f4 Nb6, when 11 Ng3 exf4 12 Bxf4 0-0 produces a position in which White's knights can't easily target e6.

10 f4 Nd7 11 g4! f5!?

In this position 11...Nb6 can be met by 12 f5, when White's space advantage is a more important factor than the bishop pair Black gets after 12...Nc4.

12 gxf5 gxf5 13 Rg1 fxe4 14 Bh3!?

Simply 14 Nxe4 would have been very dangerous for Black, whose king is looking decidedly uncomfortable.

14...Nb6! 15 Bxc8 Nc4

An important resource. 15...Rxc8 16 Bxb6! axb6 17 fxe5 dxe5 18 Nxe4 would have given White a clear advantage because of his strong knight on e4.

16 Be6+ Kh8 17 Qe1 Nxe3 18 Rxg7 Nxd1

18...Kxg7 19 Qg3+ picks up the knight on e3.

19 Rxh7+ (Diagram 6)

White has to press on with the attack, as after 19 Rxe7? Qxe7 20 Kxd1 exf4 Black's f-pawn would be a serious problem.

19...Kxh7 20 Qh4+ Kg7 21 Qg4+ Kh8

On 21...Ng6 White would play 22 f5 Qe8 23 Kxd1 when, amongst other things, he's threatening 24 Ng3.

22 Nxe4!

It looks like Black is in trouble here, though White will shortly miss the coup de grâce.

22...Ng8

If 22...exf4 23 Qh5+ Kg7 24 Ng5 Ng6 25 Qh7+ Kf6 26 Qh6 and 27 Ne4+, while 22...Qe8 is answered by 23 f5 threatening 24 Qh4+.

23 Qh5+ Kg7 24 Qg4+?

It's hard to see over the board, but 24 f5! looks good for White after 24...Qe8 25 Qg5+ Kh8 26 Qh4+ Kg7 27 N2g3, or 24...Nf6 25 Qg6+ Kh8 26 Ng5 Qe7 27 Bf7! etc.

24...Kh8 25 Qh5+ Kg7 26 Qg4+ ½-½

Game 11
☐ **A.Soltis** ■ **A.Adorjan**
Birmingham 1973

---

1 e4 g6 2 d4 Bg7 3 Nc3 d6 4 Bg5 Nc6 5 Nf3 Bg4 6 Bb5 a6 (Diagram 7)

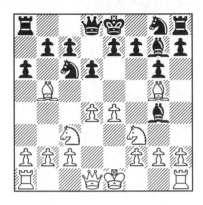

Diagram 7 (W)

Getting the bishop pair

Diagram 8 (W)

Making use of the open file

7 Bxc6+ bxc6 8 Qd3 h6

8...Bxf3 9 gxf3 Qb8 also looks very reasonable for Black. It's not clear where White's king should go.

9 Bh4 Nf6 10 h3 Bd7 11 0-0-0 Nh5 12 Qd2 g5 13 Bg3

White wants to play e4-e5, but with his opponent having a strong centre and two bishops, his position stands on feet of clay.

13...Nxg3 14 fxg3 Qb8 (Diagram 8)

 TIP: When the b-file is open it can provide an interesting way for Black to get his queen into play.

15 e5 Qb4

Black just ignores White's 'breakthrough' and gets on with his own queenside action.

16 Rhe1 Rb8 17 b3 Be6 18 g4 a5 19 Re4 Bd5 20 Re3

After 20 Nxd5 Qa3+ 21 Kb1 cxd5 22 Re2 Black can even play 22...Kd7!? to connect his rooks.

20...Be6 21 Re4 Qa3+

Disdaining the repetition.

22 Kb1 a4 23 d5

And not 23 Nxa4?? because Black can just take it.

23...axb3 24 cxb3

24 axb3? is answered by 24...Ra8, so White must capture away from the centre.

24...cxd5 25 Ra4 Qc5 26 Nxd5 dxe5 27 Ra5 Qd6 28 Qc2 (Diagram 9)

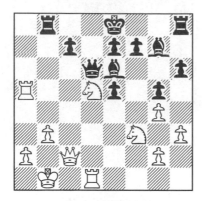

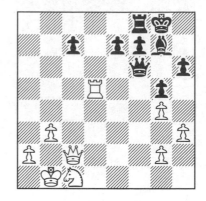

Diagram 9 (B)

Black has nothing to fear

Diagram 10 (W)

The dark squares are fatally weak

28...Bxd5

Black can even consider sacrificing his queen here: 28...0-0 29 Nf6+ (29 Nxc7 may be better, but still looks nice for Black after 29...Qb4 30 Nxe6 Qxa5 31 Nxf8 Kxf8) 29...Bxf6 30 Rxd6 cxd6 gives him wonderful compensation in the form of his mighty bishops and pawn centre.

29 Rdxd5 Qf6 30 Nxe5 0-0 31 Qf5 Qb6 32 Qf1 Qe3 33 Qf3 Qe1+ 34 Qd1 Qe4+ 35 Qc2 Qf4

Again avoiding a draw by repetition that was to be had with 35...Qe1+. In the long run Black believes that White's weakened king will tell against him.

36 Rac5 Rbd8 37 Nd3?

Probably the losing move. 37 Nd7 looks better here, the main point of which is to keep the black queen out of the f6-square, at least temporarily. Now White's troubles increase.

37...Qf1+ 38 Nc1 Qf6 39 Re5 Qb6

39...e6 also looks good.

40 Rf5 Rd6 41 Rfd5

41 Rxc7?? loses on the spot to 41...Qd4.

41...Rxd5 42 Rxd5 Qf6 (Diagram 10) 43 Qe2 e6 44 Rd2 Qa1+

With the white king getting evicted from his home one senses the beginning of the end.

45 Kc2 Be5 46 Rd7 Qc3+ 47 Kb1 Rb8 48 Rd3 Qa1+ 49 Kc2 c5 50 Kd1 c4!

Further breaking up White's position.

51 bxc4 Bf4 52 Rd2 Rb1 53 Rd8+ Kg7 0-1

Game 12
□ **A.J.Mestel** ■ **G.Botterill**
British Championship, Llanelli 1974

---

1 e4 d6 2 d4 g6 3 Nc3 Bg7 4 Bg5 Nc6 5 Bb5 a6 6 Bxc6+ bxc6 7 Nge2 Rb8 (Diagram 11)

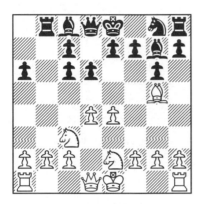

Diagram 11 (W)
Hitting the b2-pawn

Diagram 12 (W)
Creative chess

This annoying prod gets White to either weaken his queenside (with 8 b3) or forfeit castling rights with the move he chooses in the game.

8 Rb1 Nf6 9 0-0 h6 10 Bh4 g5!

> **NOTE: Exchanging White's queen's bishop with ...g6-g5 and ...Nf6-h5 is an idea worth noting. Black's dark-squared bishop becomes much more influential because it has no opponent.**

11 Bg3 Nh5 12 f4 Rb4 (Diagram 12)

The creative way in which Botterill attacks White's centre in this game deserves careful study. His pieces jump into the fray from all sorts of unusual angles.

13 Be1 Bg4! 14 Qd3 Nxf4 15 Nxf4 gxf4 16 Rxf4 h5 17 d5 Be5 18 Rf1 Qa8!

A beautiful move which would have warmed Richard Réti's heart. The queen protects c6 whilst applying more pressure to White's centre.

19 h3 Bd7 20 Nd1?

A serious mistake. White should have played 20 Qf3 immediately, when 20...f6 21 Ne2 still looks very messy.

20...Rd4 21 Qf3 cxd5 (Diagram 13)

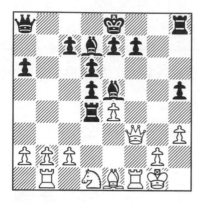

Diagram 13 (W)	**Diagram 14 (W)**
Demolishing White's centre	It's all over

22 Qxf7+

This proves to be a Pyrrhic victory as Black's king stands very well on d8.

22...Kd8 23 exd5 Qxd5 24 Bc3 Be6 25 Qf3 Qxa2 26 Bxd4 Bxd4+ 27 Nf2 Bd5 28 Qa3?

Losing. The last chance to stay on the board was with 28 Qd3.

28...Qc4 29 Kh2 Be5+ 30 Kh1 Rg8 31 Rg1 Qf4 0-1 (Diagram 14)

Summary

The aggressive side of Bc1-g5 comes packaged with some downsides. White's bishop no longer guards his queenside and would have to retreat to support the d4-square. Black can often hunt it down with ...h7-h6, ...g6-g5 and ...Nf6-h5 (leaving his own dark-squared bishop without an opponent), or even use the bishop's position to secure his centre with ...f7-f6 and ...e7-e5.

Chapter Three

Be3 and h2-h4 Systems

- Introduction
- Illustrative Games

Introduction

The original basis of the move 4 Be3 was to prepare an attack similar to the queen-side castling plan White uses against the Sicilian Dragon. White will prepare to exchange Black's dark-squared bishop with Qd2 and an eventual Bh6, prise open the h-file with h2-h4-h5, and then mate Black's castled king. Certainly this is very dangerous if Black cooperates. But I have successfully fought against this system with a plan involving a queenside expansion commencing 4...a6.

1 e4 g6 2 d4

White can, if he really wants to, play an immediate 2 h4 **(Diagram 1)** and I had a period in which I avoided this rubbish by going 1...d6 and 2...g6. Not that this is at all necessary, as Black can meet 2 h4 in several promising ways. The classic for-mula of a counterblow in the centre is seen in Galego-Davies (Game 13) in which I played 2...d5. Instead of Galego's 3 h5 White can play 3 exd5 Qxd5 4 Nc3, but this gives Black a rather good version of the Scandinavian Defence with 4...Qa5. Black might also make a gambit of it with 3 exd5 Nf6!?, again an idea borrowed from the Scandinavian, but with the moves 2 h4 and 1...g6 thrown in.

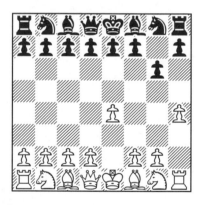

Diagram 1 (B)

Tilting at windmills

Diagram 2 (B)

Preparing Qd2

Another promising option for Black is to simply ignore White's h-pawn advance with the move 2...c5. After 3 h5 Bg7 4 d3 Nc6 5 c3 Nf6 White drove my bishop home with 6 h6 in a game Whyte-Davies, National Club Championship 1984. But after 6...Bf8 7 Bg5 d5 8 Nd2 Be6 9 Nh3 Qd7 Black nevertheless achieved a comfort-able mobilization.

I had the manic 2 Nc3 d6 3 h4 played against me by S.Leiser in the 1995 Hamburg Open, and after 3...Nf6 White sounded the charge with 4 h5 (4 d4 Bg7 transposes into the 4 h4 Nf6 line given in the notes to White's 4th move below) 4...Nxh5 5 Rxh5 gxh5 6 Qxh5. Fortunately for me I was not obliged to castle kingside, and after 6...e6 7 d4 Qf6 8 Nf3 Qg6 9 Qh2 Bd7 10 Bf4 Nc6 11 0-0-0 0-0-0 I went on to realize my extra material.

2...Bg7 3 Nc3 d6 4 Be3 (Diagram 2)

Another aggressive possibility is 4 h4 Nf6 (it makes sense to meet White's last with a developing move, regardless of the fact we're now in a Pirc Defence) 5 Be2, after which I've tended to play 5...Nc6 6 Be3 (6 d5 Ne5 7 h5 gxh5 8 Nh3 c6 9 Nf4 Bg4 10 Nxh5 Bxh5 11 Bxh5 cxd5 12 exd5 Qa5 gave Black a strong initiative in C.Boschetti-N.Davies, Lugano 1986) 6...e5 7 d5 Nd4! 8 Qd2 c6 9 0-0-0 cxd5 10 Bxd4 exd4 11 Nxd5 Nxe4 12 Bb5+ Kf8 and Black's loss of castling rights was not a significant factor in Clark-Davies, Cheshire & North Wales League 1986 (see Game 14).

4...a6

Not many people like to play such moves, but behind its odd appearance lies a great deal of logic. Black wants to expand on the queenside with the moves ...Nd7, ...b7-b5, ...Bb7 and ...c7-c5 and argues that he can attend to things like development later on. The move 4 Be3 is attuned more to attacking a castled king than one that is loitering in the centre!

5 h4

Many people choose 5 a4 at this point, but then castling queenside is no longer a real option. In Santos-Davies (Game 15) this encouraged me to provoke White still further with the ultra-flexible 5...b6!?, though in more respectable moods I have played both 5...Nf6 and 5...Nc6.

The other popular choice is 5 Qd2, after which 5...b5 is a slight inaccuracy in my opinion because 6 a4 b4 7 Nd1 leaves 7...a5 as Black's best way of defending his b-pawn. I don't like this because my plan of ...c7-c5 will give White the b5-square for his bishop. Which is why both I and Raymond Keene have played first 5...Nd7 **(Diagram 3)** here.

For example:

a) 6 f3 b5 7 Nh3 (in this position 7 a4 b4 8 Nd1 Rb8 9 Nh3 c5 10 a5 cxd4 11 Bxd4 Ngf6 12 Be2 0-0 13 0-0 Qc7 gave me a kind of super-Sicilian in M.Chandler-N.Davies, Hastings 1987/88, though I later managed to lose) 7...c5 8 dxc5 Nxc5 9 Nf2 Bb7 10 Be2 Qc7 11 a3 Rc8 12 0-0 Nf6 13 Bh6 0-0 14 Bxg7 Kxg7 15 Rae1 e5 and Black had a nice position in Rantanen-Keene, Gausdal 1979 (see Game 16).

b) 6 Nf3 b5 7 a4 b4 8 Nc2 Rb8 was seen in Szalanczy-Davies, Liechtenstein 1993 (Game 17)

5...Nf6

The right time to bring the knight out. I don't like to play 5...h5 as White can then direct his attack towards the f7- and g6-squares, bringing a knight to g5, castling kingside and using his f-pawn as a battering ram. So I only go 8...h5 once White has castled long.

6 f3 b5 7 Qd2 Bb7 8 0-0-0 h5 9 Nh3 Nbd7 10 Kb1 Rc8 (Diagram 4) 11 Qe1 e5

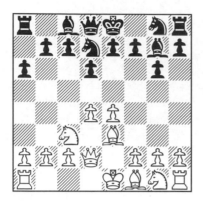

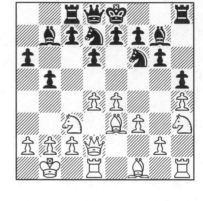

Diagram 3 (W)

Preparing ...b7-b5 and ...c7-c5

Diagram 4 (W)

Getting ready to play ...c7-c5

Black is forced to change plan as White's last move prepared to meet 11...c5 with 12 e5.

12 d5 c6 13 dxc6 Rxc6 14 Ng5 Qc7 15 Qd2

White now threatens to embarrass the rook on c6 with 16 Nd5, which was part of the reason for my next move. Regarding this sacrifice John Nunn, in his book *The Complete Pirc*, expressed a degree of scepticism and I also doubted whether it was 100 per cent sound at the time. Yet Anand was unable to find a refutation either during the game or afterwards.

As an improvement Black might consider 12...b4, driving White's knight from where it can jump to d5 before commencing undermining operations with ...c7-c6.

15...Rxc3!? 16 Qxc3 Qxc3 17 bxc3 d5 (Diagram 5)

Does Black have enough compensation here? That I don't know, but I did go on to win in Anand-Davies, Moscow 1987 (see Game 18).

Illustrative Games

Game 13
□ **L.Galego** ■ **N.Davies**
Tel Aviv 1990

1 e4 g6 2 h4 d5! (Diagram 6)

TIP: Black must never cower in the Modern. When faced with brutal aggression you have to hit back rather than retreat.

3 h5

After 3 exd5 Nf6 (3...Qxd5 is not bad either) 4 c4 c6 5 dxc6 Nxc6 Black gets superb compensation for the pawn thanks to his lead in development. And the pawn on h4 is now a weakness rather than a strength.

3...dxe4 4 hxg6 fxg6 5 Nc3 Nf6 6 Qe2

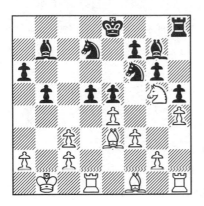

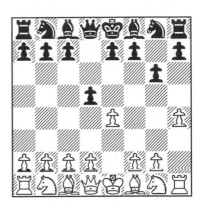

Diagram 5 (W)	Diagram 6 (W)
Black has compensation	Hitting straight back

After 6 d3 Black can simply play 6...Bf5.

6...Nc6

Returning the pawn for development.

7 Nxe4 Nxe4 8 Qxe4 Bf5 9 Qa4 a6 (Diagram 7)

9...Qd5 is an excellent alternative. In any case Black's huge lead in development gives him a clear advantage.

10 Nf3 Qd6 11 Bb5 Bxc2 12 Bxc6+ Qxc6 13 Qxc6+ bxc6 14 Rh4?!

14 Nd4 would have been a better option, though Black still has all the chances after 14...Bf5 15 Nxf5 (or 15 Nxc6 Be4) 15...gxf5 16 d3 Bg7. A pawn is a pawn, even if it's doubled and isolated.

14...Bg7 15 d4 h6 16 Ne5

Here 16 Be3 would have been better, but White wants to play actively.

16...c5! 17 Be3 g5 18 Rh3 Rd8 19 Rc1 Bf5 20 Rf3 Be4 21 Rxc5 Bxe5 22 dxe5 Bxf3 23 gxf3 Kd7 (Diagram 8)

With an extra exchange the rest is a matter of technique.

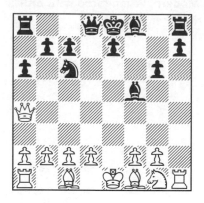

Diagram 7 (W)

Black has a clear advantage

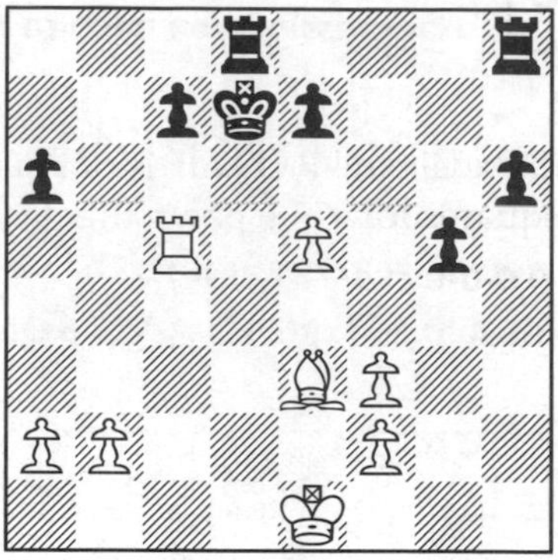

Diagram 8 (W)

And now Black is winning

24 f4 gxf4 25 Bxf4 h5 26 Kf1 Rdg8 27 Bg5 Rb8

And not 27...Rxg5 28 e6+ etc.

28 Rc2 Rb4 29 f4 Ke6 30 Rxc7 Rxb2 31 Rxe7+ Kf5 32 Rf7+ Kg4

Black's pieces are closing in on the enemy monarch.

33 Rc7 h4 34 Kg1 h3 35 Rc1 Rhb8 0-1

Game 14

□ **R.Clark** ■ **N.Davies**

Cheshire & North Wales League 1986

---

1 d4 g6 2 e4 Bg7 3 Nc3 d6 4 h4 Nf6 5 Be2 (Diagram 9)

This sharp system has been used by aggressive players such as Hungary's Gyula Sax. The 'best' response may well be 5...c5, but I usually like to counterattack d4 with ...Nc6.

5...Nc6 6 Be3

There are a couple of alternatives here:

a) 6 h5 gxh5 7 Bb5 is a sharp attempt, but then 7...a6 8 Bxc6+ bxc6 9 Nge2 Qd7 10 f3 Rg8 11 Ng3 c5! 12 dxc5 Qc6 gave Black excellent counterplay in A.Ribas-P.Zarnicki, Buenos Aires 1991.

b) 6 d5 Ne5 7 h5 gxh5 8 Nh3 c6 9 Nf4 Bg4 10 Nxh5 Bxh5 11 Bxh5 cxd5 12 exd5 Qa5 gave Black a strong initiative in C.Boschetti-N.Davies, Lugano 1986.

6...e5 7 d5 Nd4!

NOTE: 7...Nd4! is a thematic pawn sacrifice aimed at depriving White of his dark-squared bishop.

8 Qd2

After 8 Bxd4 exd4 9 Qxd4 0-0 I believe that Black will have excellent play on the dark squares for his sacrificed pawn.

8...c6 9 0-0-0 cxd5 10 Bxd4

After 10 exd5 one good way for Black to get a good game is with 10...Nxe2+ 11 Ngxe2 Ng4, trying to eliminate White's other bishop as well whilst releasing the f-pawn for a possible advance.

10...exd4 11 Nxd5 Nxe4 12 Bb5+ Kf8 (Diagram 10)

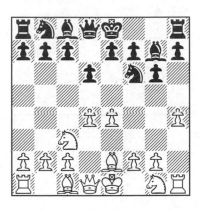

Diagram 9 (B)

A sharp system

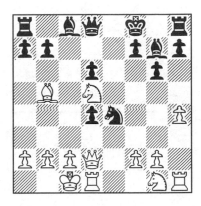

Diagram 10 (W)

A minor inconvenience

Black gives up castling rights, but he has two bishops and an extra pawn. Instead, 12...Bd7 13 Bxd7+ Qxd7 is bad because of 14 Re1, though Black could consider re-capturing on d7 with the king.

13 Qf4 Nc5 14 Nf3 Ne6 15 Qe4 a6 16 Bc4 Bd7 17 Rhe1 Rc8 18 Bb3

Perhaps 18 Nxd4 would have been a stronger option, though Black clearly has the better of it after 18...Rxc4 (and not 18...Nxd4 19 Rxd4 Bxd4 20 Qxd4 Rg8 21 Nf6, when suddenly the tables are turned) 19 Nxe6+ fxe6 20 Qxc4 exd5 21 Qxd5 Bc6, for example 22 Qxd6+ Qxd6 23 Rxd6 Bxg2 etc.

18...Nc5 19 Qf4 Bf5 (Diagram 11) 20 Rd2 d3?!

It might have been wiser to play 20...Ne6, for example 21 Rxe6 Bxe6 22 Nxd4 Bxd5 23 Bxd5 Qf6 with a clear advantage.

21 c3 Be6 22 Ng5?

The losing move. During the game I probably assumed that 22 Bc4 was answered by 22...b5 (22...Kg8 is a stronger move), but then 23 Ng5 puts a cat amongst the pigeons because 23...Bf5? runs into 24 Re7!.

22...Nxb3+ 23 axb3 Bxd5 24 Rxd3 Bxb3?!

24...h6 is even stronger.

25 Qb4 Bh6 26 Rxd6 Bxg5+ 27 hxg5?

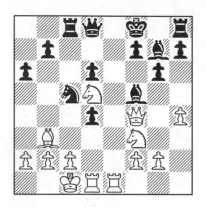

Diagram 11 (W)

Taking aim at c2

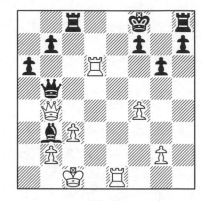

Diagram 12 (W)

White falls apart

27 Kb1 was better, when Black has to settle for having an assortment of pieces for his queen after 27...Qe7! 28 Rxe7 Bxe7 29 Qxb7 Bxd6 30 Qxc8+ Kg7. Now it starts to get easy.

27...Qxg5+ 28 f4?

White is falling apart. 28 Rd2+ was relatively best.

28...Qb5 (Diagram 12) 29 Rd8+ Kg7 30 Qd4+ f6 31 Rd6 Rhf8 32 Re7+ Kg8 0-1

Game 15
☐ L.Santos ■ N.Davies
Portugal 1987

---

1 d4 g6 2 e4 Bg7 3 Nc3 d6 4 Be3 a6 5 a4

Trying to stop ...b7-b5, but whenever White plays this move it's going to be a lot riskier for him to castle queenside. This is one of the effects of ...a7-a6 in the Modern: prophylaxis against 0-0-0.

5...b6 6 Be2 Bb7 7 Nf3 Nd7 8 0-0 e6 (Diagram 13)

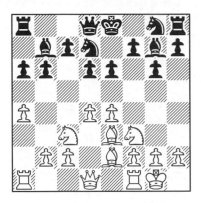

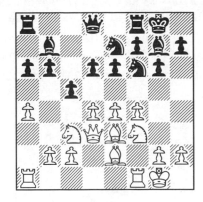

Diagram 13 (W)

Another Hippopotamus set-up

Diagram 14 (W)

The key pawn lever

Going for a Hippopotamus set-up, which is always difficult for White to get to grips with. In the game he goes for f2-f4, getting positions akin to the Austrian Attack. But then White loses a lot of time moving his knight from f3 and back.

9 Nd2

Another idea is 9 Qd2 getting ready to play Be3-h6 should Black move his knight from g8. A.Pimenta-A.Shchekachev, Metz 1998, continued 9...h6 (stopping White's plan and preparing a possible ...g6-g5) 10 h3 Ne7 11 Bf4 Nf6 (I would be tempted to play 11...g5!? followed by 12...Ng6) 12 Bd3 g5 13 Be3 d5 14 exd5 Nexd5 15 Nxd5 Nxd5 16 c3 Qd6 17 Qe2 0-0 18 Rfe1 c5 with a comfortable game for Black.

9...Ne7 10 f4 0-0 11 Nf3

In the game J.Yrjola-Z.Sturua, Helsinki 1992, White varied with 11 Bf3, but after 11...d5 12 e5 Nf5 13 Bf2 c5 14 Ne2 Qc7 15 c3 f6 Black was setting about undermining White's pawn centre and obtained excellent counterplay.

11...Nf6

With White's knight leaving d2, the e4-pawn is now vulnerable.

12 Qd3 c5! (Diagram 14) 13 dxc5 bxc5 14 Rfd1 Ng4 15 Bc1 d5! (Diagram 15)

Now that White's bishop has left e3, this is very strong

16 h3 c4! 17 Qd2 Qb6+ 18 Nd4 e5?

The simple 18...Nc6! would have been stronger, the point being that 19 Bxg4 (19 hxg4 Nxd4 20 Kh1 dxe4 is no better) 19...Bxd4+ 20 Kh1 dxe4 21 Nxe4? loses a piece after 21...f5.

19 fxe5 Nxe5 20 a5 Qc7 21 exd5 Nd3!? 22 cxd3?!

22 Qe3 was preferable.

22...Bxd4+ 23 Kh1 Nf5 24 Ne4 Bxd5 25 Qf4 Qe7 26 Bf3 Rad8 27 Ng3 Nxg3+ 28 Qxg3 Be5 29 Qf2 Bxf3 30 Qxf3 Rxd3 31 Rxd3 cxd3 32 Qxd3 Rd8 33 Qe2?

Cracking under the strain. 33 Qf1 would have been better, so as to meet 33...Bb8 with 34 Bf4. After the text White can no longer defend along the h2-b8 diagonal.

33...Bb8! (Diagram 16) 34 Qf1 Qe5 35 Kg1 Ba7+ 36 Kh1 Bb8

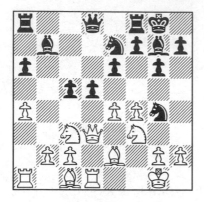

Diagram 15 (W)

Striking again in the centre

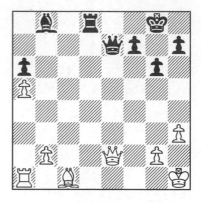

Diagram 16 (W)

White has no defence

Gaining time on the clock.

37 Kg1 Qh2+ 38 Kf2 Qg3+ 39 Kg1 Re8 40 Ra3 Ba7+ 0-1

Game 16
☐ **Y.Rantanen** ◼ **R.Keene**
Gausdal 1979

---

1 e4 g6 2 d4 Bg7 3 Nc3 d6 4 Be3 a6 5 Qd2 Nd7! (Diagram 17)

I, too, prefer this move to the immediate 5...b5, but there are a lot of strong players who don't see the problem. For example 6 a4 b4 7 Nd1 a5 8 c3 bxc3 9 bxc3 Nf6 10 f3 0-0 11 Bd3 Ba6 12 Ne2 Nbd7 13 0-0 Nb6 14 Bxa6 Rxa6 15 Qd3 Ra8 16 Bf2 Qd7 17 Nb2 Rfb8 was fine for Black in V.Anand-Z.Azmaiparashvili, Dubai 2002. So the exclamation mark may be somewhat subjective!

6 f3 b5 7 Nh3

In this position 7 a4 can be answered by 7...b4 8 Nd1 Rb8, which is only possible if the knight has gone to d7 first.

7...c5! (Diagram 18)

It makes sense to play this before putting the bishop on b7 in case White manages to shut the bishop out of play with d4-d5. Indeed, an earlier game of Keene's had gone 7...Bb7 8 Be2 c5 9 d5!, posing some challenges to Black in W.Hartston-R.Keene, British Championship, Brighton 1972.

Diagram 17 (W)

An important finesse

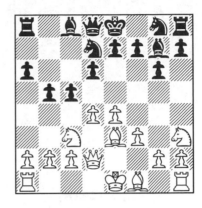

Diagram 18 (W)

Another accurate move

8 dxc5?!

White can play 8 d5 in this position, too, but then Black's light-squared bishop is on a better diagonal.

8...Nxc5 9 Nf2

9 Bxc5 dxc5 10 Qxd8+ Kxd8 11 0-0-0+ Bd7 12 Nd5 Rb8 is simply better for Black thanks to his bishop pair.

9...Bb7 10 Be2 Qc7 11 a3

After 11 Nd5 Bxd5 12 Qxd5 Rc8 13 c3 Na4!, the threats of ...Nxb2 and ...Nxc3 are awkward for White.

11...Rc8 12 0-0 Nf6 13 Bh6 0-0 14 Bxg7 Kxg7 15 Rae1 e5! (Diagram 19)

Staking out the dark squares and emphasizing the fact that Black has the better bishop.

16 Bd3 Ne6 17 g3?! Rfd8 18 f4

This plan, initiated by White's previous move, is very risky due to the damage caused to his kingside.

18...exf4 19 gxf4 d5! 20 e5 Ne4!

Sacrificing a pawn to open White's position up.

21 Nfxe4 dxe4 22 Nxe4 Nc5 23 Nxc5 Qxc5+ 24 Qf2 Rd4! (Diagram 20)

The point behind Black's 20th move, threatening both 25...Rxf4 and 25...Qd5.

25 Re2?

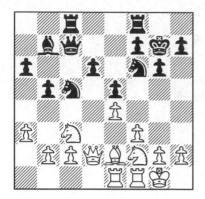

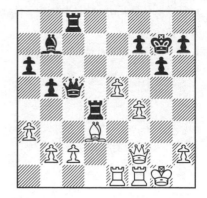

Diagram 19 (W)

Staking out the dark squares

Diagram 20 (W)

Threatening ...Rxf4 and ...Qd5

The losing move. White had to play 25 Re3, when 25...Qd5 26 Qg3 Rxd3! 27 cxd3 (if 27 Rxd3? Qh1+ 28 Kf2 Rxc2+ 29 Ke1 Rc1+ wins on the spot) 27...Rc2 28 Ref3 Rxb2 29 Qg5 intending f4-f5 may well be enough to draw. A sample line is 29...Kg8 30 Qe7 Qd4+ 31 R3f2 Rxf2 32 Rxf2 Qd5 33 Re2 Qd4+ 34 Kf1 Qxf4+ 35 Rf2 Qc1+ 36 Ke2 Qc2+ 37 Ke3 Qc1+ 38 Kd4 Qa1+ with a draw by perpetual check.

25...Rxf4 26 Qxc5 Rg4+ 27 Kf2 Rg2+ 28 Ke3 Rxe2+ 29 Kd4 Rxc5 30 Kxc5 Rxe5+ 31 Kb6 Bc8 32 a4?

Either 32 c4 or 32 Rf4 offers more chances.

32...bxa4 33 c4 Re3 34 Rd1 Bg4 35 Rd2 Re6+ 36 Ka7?

36 Kc5 was the only way to stay on the board.

36...Re7+ 37 Kxa6 Rd7 38 Kb5 Bf5 39 Kxa4 Rxd3 40 Rxd3 Bxd3 0-1

Game 17
□ **E.Szalanczy** ■ **N.Davies**
Liechtenstein 1993

---

1 e4 g6 2 d4 Bg7 3 Nc3 d6 4 Be3 a6 5 Qd2 Nd7 6 Nf3 b5 7 a4 b4 8 Ne2 (Diagram 21)

8 Nd5 is an attempt to actually refute Black's play and I had two games continue with 8...Ngf6 9 Qxb4 Nxe4 10 Qa5 Ra7 11 Nb4 Bb7 12 Bb5. The first of these (L.Barczay-N.Davies, Budapest 1988) went 12...Ra8 and draw! In the second (J.Dobos-N.Davies, Hastings 1994/95) I found the superior 12...Qc8 after some 26 minutes thought. Following 13 Bc6 0-0 14 0-0 Ndf6 15 Rfe1 e6 Black's extra central

pawn gives him a tiny pull.

8...Rb8

This is one of the joys of playing ...Nb8-d7 before ...b7-b5: the b-pawn can be defended by the rook. 8...a5 is less good because it gives White the b5-square.

Diagram 21 (B)

The knight heads for the kingside

Diagram 22 (W)

Keeping the c-file closed

9 Ng3 c5 10 Bd3 cxd4 11 Nxd4 Qc7 12 0-0 h5!?

I must admit that this may not be everyone's cup of tea, attacking White with most of Black's pieces on the back rank. For those with weak stomachs there are solid alternatives in 12...Nc5 and 12...Ngf6.

13 Rfc1 h4 14 Nge2 Ngf6 15 c3 b3 (Diagram 22) 16 f3 d5

WARNING: Be careful about trying this kind of thing at home. Black must always think twice about opening the centre with his king uncastled, though in this case I believe I had it all more or less under control.

Black can win a piece at this point with 16...e5, but White gets compensation after 17 Qd1 exd4 (17...Nc5!? may be better) 18 cxd4 Qb7 19 Bf4, hitting d6.

17 exd5 Nxd5 18 Re1

Anticipating 18...e5 (trapping the knight on d4), White places his rook opposite the black king.

18...e5 19 Bf2 0-0 20 Nxb3

In such a complex position it's often difficult to pinpoint the exact turning point, but this might well be it. White now finds himself with inadequate compensation, whereas after 20 Be4 he is still fighting. Actually I still prefer Black after 20...N5f6

21 Nc6 Nxe4 22 Ne7+ Kh7 23 fxe4 Nf6 24 Nxc8 Nxe4, but this isn't easy to see when there are so many fascinating alternatives.

20...Rxb3 21 Bxg6 N7f6

Not 21...fxg6?? because of 22 Qxd5+, picking up the rook on b7.

22 Bb1 Qb7 23 Bxh4 Rxb2 24 Qg5 Nh7 25 Qc1 Be6 26 Bd3 Rc8? (Diagram 23)

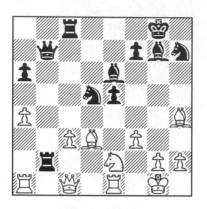

Diagram 23 (W)	**Diagram 24 (W)**
Giving White a chance	Black has a decisive attack

A bad slip, after which things become chaotic again. Simply 26...Rb8 would have kept control.

27 Bxa6! Qxa6 28 Qxb2 e4! 29 fxe4 Nxc3 30 Nxc3 Bxc3 31 Qb5 Qa8 32 a5?

With time trouble looming White drops his e4-pawn. Black is better again.

32...Bxa1 33 Rxa1 Qxe4 34 Bf2 Bd5 35 Qf1 Ng5 (Diagram 24)

Suddenly it is Black who has the attack, his pieces converging on the light squares around White's king.

36 Re1 Nf3+ 37 gxf3 Qxf3 38 Bg3 Qh1+ 39 Kf2 Rc2+ 40 Ke3 Qe4 mate

---

Game 18
☐ **V.Anand** ■ **N.Davies**
Moscow 1987

---

1 e4 d6 2 d4 g6 3 Nc3 Bg7 4 Be3 a6 5 h4 Nf6 6 f3 b5 7 Qd2 Bb7

Another option is 7...h5, intending to take White's knight off should it try to go to g5 via h3. A game E.Berg-T.Hillarp Persson, Swedish Team Championship 2005, continued 8 0-0-0 c6 9 Nh3 Bxh3 10 Rxh3 Nbd7 11 Kb1 Qc7 12 Rh1 Rc8 with a reasonable position for Black at this point.

8 0-0-0 h5 9 Nh3 Nbd7 (Diagram 25)

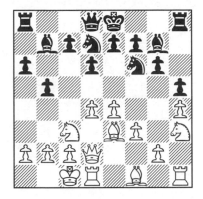
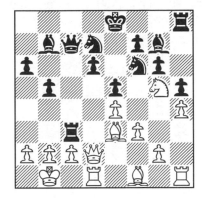

Diagram 25 (W)	**Diagram 26 (W)**
Preparing the standard ...c7-c5	An ambitious sacrifice

10 Kb1

White can also play 10 Ng5, for example 10...0-0 11 g4 Rc8?! (11...c5 looks better to me) 12 gxh5 Nxh5 13 Bh3 e6 14 Rhg1 Qf6 15 Bg4 and Black was in trouble on the kingside in V.Inkiov-N.Sanchez, Condom 2002.

10...Rc8 11 Qe1

Getting ready to meet 11...c5 with 12 e5. For this reason Black needs to change plan.

WARNING: Black must avoid playing routinely in the Modern.

11...e5 12 d5 c6

12...Nb6 is another possibility for Black, keeping open the option of ...c7-c6 whilst introducing a new one in ...b5-b4 followed by ...a6-a5.

13 dxc6 Rxc6 14 Ng5 Qc7!?

The other move to be considered is just 14...0-0 and then if 15 Qd2 Black can play 15...Nb6. The text envisages an exchange sacrifice on c3.

15 Qd2 Rxc3!? (Diagram 26)

TIP: Normally this exchange sacrifice is good if Black gets at least a pawn for it. Here it is more controversial.

16 Qxc3

Of course 16 bxc3?! d5 would involve much more danger for the white king because of the presence of queens.

16...Qxc3 17 bxc3 d5 18 exd5 Nxd5 19 Bd2 N7f6 20 Ne4?!

White might consider an immediate 20 c4!?, though Black is not without compensation after 20...bxc4 21 Bxc4 0-0.

20...0-0 (Diagram 27)

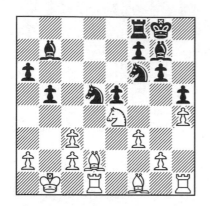

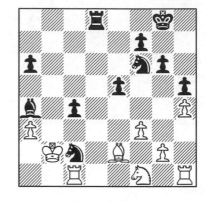

Diagram 27 (W)

Black has good compensation

Diagram 28 (B)

After this Black is winning

20...Nxe4 looks playable, both here and at several later stages (see the following notes). I had a tendency to reject such ideas because they'd inhibit the action of my 'Modern' bishop on g7.

21 c4 bxc4 22 Ba5 Bc6?

Better was 22...Nxe4 23 fxe4 Ne3 24 Re1 Nxf1 25 Rhxf1 f5, with at least equality for Black.

23 a3?

Neither side is playing too well in this messy position. White can punish Black's previous move with 23 Nxf6+ Bxf6 24 Bxc4 Rb8+ 25 Kc1.

23...Rb8+ 24 Ka2 Ba4?

24...Nxe4 25 fxe4 Ne3 is good for Black here.

25 Rc1?

And White should again play 25 Nxf6+ Nxf6 26 Bxc4.

25...Bh6

Black is still better after 25...Nxe4 26 fxe4 Bh6.

26 Bd2 Bxd2 27 Nxd2 Ne3 28 Be2 Rd8

I should probably have protected my c4-pawn with 28...Bb5, and White in turn should have taken it.

29 Nf1?! Nxc2 30 Kb2? (Diagram 28)

30 Bxc4 was correct and, after 30...Nd5, simplifying with 31 Bxd5. It would probably have been a draw this way.

30...c3+! 31 Ka2

If 31 Kxc3 Nd5+ 32 Kc4 Nd4 wins, while 32 Kb2 Rb8+ leads to mate.

31...Nd4 32 Bd3 Bb3+ 33 Ka1 Nd5 34 Be4 Ne2 35 Bxd5 Rxd5 36 Re1 Nd4 37 Rc1

37 Ne3 Ra5 is no better.

37...Ne2

37...Nc2+ would also win.

38 Re1 Rd3 0-1

White is completely tied up and my next move will be 39...c2.

Young Anand was evidently not happy with the outcome of this game and has
since been dodging me by playing in category 18+ events.

Summary

The development of White's bishop on e3 has traditionally been associated with
Qd1-d2, castling long and throwing the h-pawn up the board. The problem is that
Black hasn't yet declared his king position and can build up his own attack on the
queenside with ...a7-a6, ...b7-b5, ...Nb8-d7 and ...c7-c5, whilst leaving his king in
the middle. White's pieces are not that well equipped to answer this with a central
breakthrough.

Accordingly there has been a gradual switch to a quieter plan based on Ng1-f3,
Bf1-d3 and castling short. Black needs to play accurately against this set-up, but if
he does so he gets good counterplay. My game against Szalanczy (Game 17) is a
good illustration of the potential in Black's position.

Chapter Four

Bc4 Systems

■ **Introduction**

■ **Illustrative Games**

Introduction

In the early days of the Pirc and Modern Defences putting a bishop on c4 was one of White's most popular treatments. No doubt he was hoping to exploit Black's slow development with a quick attack against f7, and with inaccurate play by Black disasters did occur.

 WARNING: The game 1 e4 g6 2 d4 Bg7 3 Nf3 d6 4 Bc4 Nd7?? 5 Bxf7+! Kxf7 6 Ng5+ Ke8 7 Ne6 1-0 (Diagram 1) has cropped up a number of times!

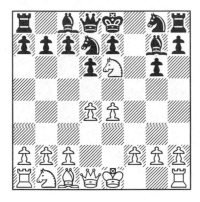

Diagram 1 (B)

Whoops!

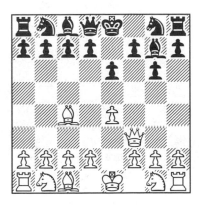

Diagram 2 (W)

Not this time

Of course Black does not need to be so cooperative, and if he avoids such accidents the bishop on c4 is not very effectively placed. The Bc4 systems have drifted out of fashion, though they are still quite popular at club and county level.

1 e4 g6 2 d4

I have had 2 Bc4 played against me several times, once even by Mark Hebden in the 1986 Upminster Open. This (Game 20) continued 2...Bg7 3 Qf3 e6 **(Diagram 2)** 4 c3 Ne7 5 d4 d5 6 Bd3, and now if I could have my time over again I'd probably play 6...dxe4 7 Bxe4 c5 with very strong counterplay.

A number of players have, after 3...e6, sacrificed a pawn against me with 4 d4, the so-called "Monkey's Bum Attack", which I believe was first analysed in Streatham in South London. I have always taken this pawn and always won, Newton-Davies (Game 19) being a nice example. The secret of defending these positions is not to go beyond the third rank too early and especially not with pawns.

2...Bg7 3 Nc3

White can also bring his other knight out with 3 Nf3, but there too Black should answer with 3...d6 4 Bc4 e6, making White's c4-bishop bite on granite, and then going for a Hippopotamus style set-up. Kochyev-Romanishin, Leningrad 1977, continued 5 Bg5 Ne7 6 Bb3 h6 7 Be3 d5 8 Nbd2 b6 9 0-0 dxe4 10 Nxe4 Bb7 with good counterplay for Black (see Game 21).

3...d6 4 Bc4 e6! (Diagram 3)

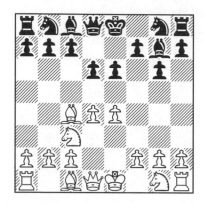

Diagram 3 (W)	**Diagram 4 (W)**
Blunting the c4-bishop	A typical Hippopotamus concept

A key move, blunting the effects of the bishop on c4. I used to like 4...Nc6 in this position (see, for example, my game against Gausel), but after 5 Nf3 Nf6 there's a transposition into the Pirc Defence.

5 Nf3

White can also play in Austrian Attack style with 5 f4, but Black obtained good counterplay after 5...Ne7 6 Nf3 a6 7 0-0 0-0 8 Bb3 b5 9 a4 b4 10 Ne2 Nd7 11 Qe1 a5 12 Qh4 Ba6 13 Re1 c5 in Del Rio Angelis-Spraggett, Mondariz 1998 (Game 22).

5...Ne7 6 Bg5 h6 7 Bh4 a6 8 0-0 Nd7 9 Qe2 g5 10 Bg3 Ng6 (Diagram 4) 11 e5 g4

and Black took the e5-pawn for insufficient compensation in Sabitov-Petrosian, Moscow 1983 (Game 23).

Illustrative Games

Game 19
☐ **R.Newton** ■ **N.Davies**
British Championship, Morecambe 1981

1 e4 g6 2 Bc4 Bg7 3 Qf3 e6 4 d4 (Diagram 5)

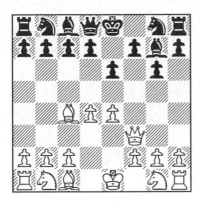

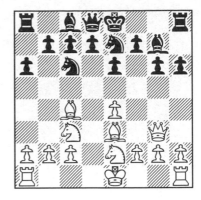

Diagram 5 (B)

The "Monkey's Bum Attack"

Diagram 6 (W)

Discouraging long castling

This Morra Gambit style pawn sacrifice had a brief period of popularity. White hopes that the piece play and lead in development he obtains will be sufficient compensation, but the problem he will have is in creating a breach in Black's position without it costing too much.

4...Bxd4 5 Ne2 Bg7 6 Nbc3 Nc6 7 Qg3

Another example is J.Bellon Lopez-L.Vadasz, Karlovac 1979, which continued 7 Bf4 d6 8 0-0-0 Bd7 9 g4 a6 10 h4 Qe7 11 g5 0-0-0 (I don't consider this to be very necessary, and it even gives White a target) 12 Qe3 h6 13 Bg3 hxg5 14 hxg5 Rxh1 15 Rxh1 Qf8 16 a3 Nge7 17 b4 Kb8 with nebulous compensation for White.

7...Nge7

Black has other possibilities in 7...Nf6 and 7...d6. In either case I think White should struggle to get enough compensation.

8 Bg5 h6 9 Be3 a6 (Diagram 6)

By now readers should be well aware of my usage of this move to discourage queenside castling.

10 a4 b6 11 0-0 Bb7 12 Rad1 d6 13 f4 Rg8!

Pointing the rook at White's queen and king. The idea is to prepare ...g6-g5 and gain both the open g-file and the e5-square.

14 Rd2 Qd7 15 Rb1

Evidently looking forward to my castling long, after which he'd charge his b-pawn forward. But castling isn't necessary yet.

15...g5! (Diagram 7)

Diagram 7 (W)

Initiating kingside counterplay

Diagram 8 (B)

Time for the dénouement

One of the joys of being a pawn up is that you can often return it in order to gain the initiative.

 NOTE: This pawn sacrifice is analogous to the ...b7-b5 ideas we have if White has castled queenside, although it is much rarer because Black will often want to castle kingside himself.

16 fxg5 hxg5 17 Nd4

After 17 Bxg5 Ne5 18 Bb3 Bh6 19 h4 0-0-0, the initiative would be firmly in Black's hands. So White decides not to recover his pawn, but Black gets the initiative anyway.

17...Be5 18 Qg4 Nxd4 19 Bxd4 Bxd4+ 20 Rxd4 Nc6 21 Rd2 Ne5 22 Qe2 g4 23 Kh1 Qe7 24 Re1?

24 Rf1 would have been better, as now White can't play g2-g3 without having his rooks forked with ...Nf3.

24...Rh8 25 Qf1 (Diagram 8)

25 g3 Nf3 just wins the exchange.

25...Rxh2+!! 26 Kxh2 Qh4+ 27 Kg1 g3 28 Bb5+

Trying desperately to make room for White's king on e2, but after my reply he must give up his queen.

28...Ke7 29 Qc4 Nxc4 30 Bxc4 Qg5 31 Rd4 Rh8 32 e5 Rh1+!

I admit that I was showing off at this point.

33 Kxh1 Qh6+ 34 Kg1 Qh2+ 35 Kf1 Qxg2 mate

Game 20
□ **M.Hebden** ■ **N.Davies**
Upminster 1986

1 e4 g6 2 Bc4 Bg7 3 Qf3 e6 4 c3 (Diagram 9)

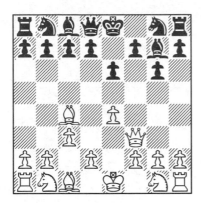

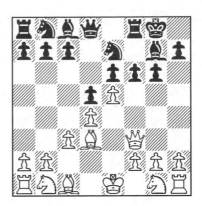

Diagram 9 (B)

Preparing d2-d4

Diagram 10 (W)

Attacking the pawn front

The wily Hebden does not give away pawns lightly.

4...Ne7

Preparing ...d7-d5. After 4...c5 5 d4 cxd4 6 cxd4 Bxd4 7 Ne2 Bg7 8 Nbc3 White would have much better compensation than in the previous game because there are more open lines.

5 d4 d5 6 Bd3 0-0

In retrospect it would have been better to play 6...dxe4 7 Bxe4 c5! 8 dxc5 (8 Bxb7 Bxb7 9 Qxb7 Nbc6 10 dxc5 Rb8 11 Qa6 Ne5 would give Black a vitriolic initiative) 8...Nd7, inviting White to try and hold on to the pawn with b2-b4, after which ...a7-a5 would wreak havoc on the queenside.

7 e5 f6 (Diagram 10)

The pawn chain is undermined at the head rather than the base, though Nimzowitsch would not have altogether approved.

8 exf6 Bxf6 9 Bh6 Rf7 10 Qg3 c5! 11 dxc5 e5! (Diagram 11)

Playing for the initiative rather than counting the cost in pawns.

12 Bg5 Nf5 13 Bxf5 Bxf5 14 Bxf6 Qxf6 15 Nf3 Nd7 16 0-0 Raf8 17 Nbd2 Bd3 18 Ng5 Bxf1 19 Nxf7 Rxf7 20 Rxf1 Nxc5

Black is pushing here because of his pawn centre and pressure on the f-file. But Hebden finds a good plan.

21 c4! Qf4

Black prepares the advance ...e5-e4. Instead, 21...d4 22 b4 would give White's d2-knight access to the e4-square.

22 Nf3?!

A better line is 22 Qxf4 Rxf4 23 cxd5 Rd4 24 Nb1 Rxd5 25 Rc1, when it's starting to look drawish.

22...Qxg3 23 hxg3 e4 24 Nd2 Rd7 (Diagram 12)

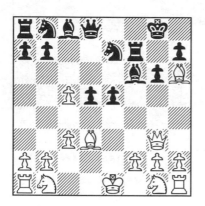

Diagram 11 (W)

Playing for the initiative

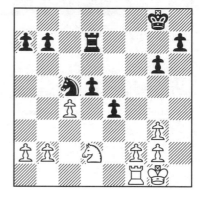

Diagram 12 (W)

Letting White off the hook

Here 24...d4! 25 b4 Nd3 26 Nxe4 Nxb4 is better for Black.

25 b4 dxc4 26 Nxc4 Rd4 27 bxc5 Rxc4 28 Rb1 Rxc5 29 Rxb7 Rc1+ 30 Kh2 Rc2 31 Rxa7 Rxf2 32 g4 e3 33 Kg3 Rf1 34 Re7 ½-½

34...Ra1 35 Rxe3 Rxa2 is about as drawn as you can get.

Game 21
□ **A.Kochyev** ■ **O.Romanishin**
Leningrad 1977

---

1 e4 g6 2 d4 Bg7 3 Nf3 d6 4 Bc4 e6! (Diagram 13)

I think this is an excellent plan, immediately blunting the action of White's c4-bishop. Modern Defence practitioners should have the line 4...Nd7?? 5 Bxf7+! etched into their hide, after which the attractions of 4...e6 become very much clearer.

5 Bg5

Instead, 5 Nc3 transposes to Game 23, Sabitov-Petrosian.

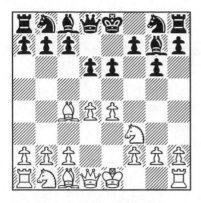

Diagram 13 (W)

Blunting the c4-bishop

Diagram 14 (W)

Black has a good position

In R.Hübner-T.V.Petrosian, Biel Interzonal 1976, White played 5 Bb3 Ne7 6 0-0 0-0 7 c3 b6 8 Nbd2 Nbc6?! (8...c5! was better, to attack the centre at once) 9 Re1 Na5 10 Bc2 c5 11 Nf1 Nac6 12 Be3 when he was slightly better and should later have won.

In this line Black should probably delay castling with 6...b6, for example 7 Bf4 Bb7 8 Re1 Nd7 9 c3 h6 10 Na3 0-0 11 Qd3 Nc6 12 Rad1 Qe7 13 h3 Rad8 14 Bh2 a6 15 Nc4 b5 16 Ncd2 Nb6 with a tense and complex position which Black eventually won in W.Wittmann-S.Kindermann, Munich 1987. Admittedly White has a space edge, but as Nunn pointed out in *The Complete Pirc*: "Black doesn't play like this in order to equalize from the opening."

One final example is G.Agzamov-M.Todorcevic, Belgrade 1982, in which White played 5 0-0 and obtained his "slight advantage" from the opening after 5...Ne7 6 c3 Nd7 7 Re1 h6 8 Bb3 b6 9 Nbd2 Bb7 10 Nc4 a6 11 h3. Once again let me say that Black doesn't play the Modern Defence in order to get clean theoretical equality from the opening!.

5...Ne7 6 Bb3 h6 7 Be3

In their notes in *Informator*, Romanishin and Mikhalchishin suggested 7 Bf4!? as a possible improvement. It is often difficult to reach any firm conclusions in the muddy and unexplored waters of the Modern Defence.

7...d5 8 Nbd2

According to Romanishin, Black is also slightly better after 8 e5 b6 9 0-0 Nf5.

8...b6 9 0-0 dxe4 10 Nxe4 Bb7 11 Ng3 0-0 (Diagram 14) 12 Qe2

White may have done better to shut Black's knight out of d5 with 12 c4!?, before following with Qe2 and Rad1. As the game goes he drifts into a passive position, and the problems grow when he creates weaknesses.

12...Nd5 13 Bd2 Nc6 14 Rad1 Na5 15 Ba4

Although this looks awkward it is probably better than surrendering the bishop pair. 15 c3 Nxb3 16 axb3 a5! is just good for Black.

15...Qf6! 16 b4?!

In view of the initiative Black gains with his 18th move this weakening of the queenside should really have been avoided if possible. 16 Ne4 was stronger.

16...Nc6 17 Ne4 Qe7 18 a3 a5 19 Qc4 Na7! (Diagram 15)

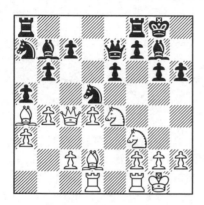

Diagram 15 (W)

A very clever move

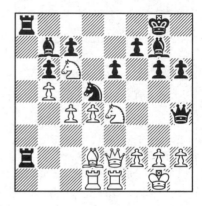

Diagram 16 (B)

The decisive mistake

A very clever move by the creative Romanishin. After 20 bxa5 the idea is 20...b5! 21 Bxb5 Nxb5 22 Qxb5 Ba6, winning the exchange for inadequate compensation. Black might also consider 20...Qxa3!? when White's pieces look rather loose.

As the game goes there are no such complications, just clear and simple pressure for Black.

20 Rfe1 axb4 21 axb4 Rfd8 22 b5 Nc8 23 Bb3 Nd6 24 Qe2

Already Black has a definite edge. 24 Nxd6 cxd6 25 Qe2 Qf6 is no better.

24...Nf5 25 c3 Ra3 26 Bc4 Nd6! 27 Ne5 Nxc4

Black had to be careful at this stage. Superficially it seems that 27...Nxe4 28 Qxe4 Rxc3? 29 Bxc3 Nxc3 30 Qxb7 Bxe5 is good for him, but this unfortunately runs into 29 Nxg6!. Such is the balance between victory and defeat in chess; one false step can spell disaster.

28 Qxc4 Rda8 29 Nc6 Qh4 30 Qe2 Ra2 31 c4? (Diagram 16)

The decisive mistake, probably influence by a degree of time pressure. He should have played 31 Qf3.

31...Bxc6 32 bxc6 Nb4

White can no longer defend his pawn weaknesses and the rest is a relatively simple mopping up operation.

33 g3 Qd8 34 d5 exd5 35 cxd5 Nc2 36 d6 cxd6 37 Rf1 Nd4 38 Qc4 d5 39 c7 dxc4 40 cxd8Q+ Rxd8 0-1

Game 22
□ **S.Del Rio Angelis** ■ **K.Spraggett**
Mondariz 1998

---

1 d4 d6 2 e4 g6 3 Nc3 Bg7 4 Bc4 e6 5 f4 (Diagram 17)

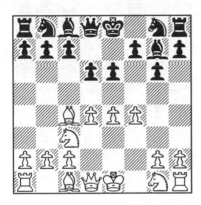

Diagram 17 (B)

A quasi-Austrian Attack

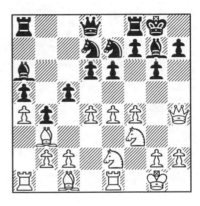

Diagram 18 (W)

No time to delay

Giving the position an Austrian Attack flavour. In fact it could have been reached via 4 f4 e6 5 Bc4 or 5 Nf3 Ne7 6 Bc4.

5...Ne7 6 Nf3

White can take the sting out of a possible ...d6-d5 with 6 Bb3, but then 6...b6 7 Nf3 Bb7 8 0-0 0-0 9 Qe1 d5 10 e5 c5 11 a4 Nbc6 12 Be3 Nf5 13 Rd1 cxd4 14 Nxd4 Nfxd4 15 Bxd4 Nxd4 16 Rxd4 f6 was good for Black in S.Johnsen-T.Ernst, Gausdal 1994.

6...a6

6...d5 is also a good idea as it leads to the break-up of White's pawn centre. After 7 Be2 dxe4 8 Nxe4 Nf5 9 c3 0-0 10 Qc2 b6 11 Bd2 Bb7 12 Bd3 Nd7 13 0-0-0 (thus far R.Zell-A.Kraeussling, Unterfranken 1988), Black can achieve at least equality with

13...c5.

7 0-0 0-0 8 Bb3 b5 9 a4 b4 10 Ne2 Nd7 11 Qe1

Playing for the attack, but White's position stands on feet of clay.

11...a5 12 Qh4 Ba6 13 Re1 c5 (Diagram 18) 14 Be3

Black's reply gives him the better game. The critical line was 14 f5, which Black should meet with 14...gxf5! (14...exf5 15 Bg5 Re8 16 Bd5 Rc8 17 Nf4 is very dangerous) 15 Bg5 Ng6, for example 16 Bxd8 Nxh4 17 Bxh4 fxe4 18 Ng5 d5 and Black will soon have three pawns for the sacrificed piece.

14...Nc6 15 Qh3

White's 'best' might have been 15 Qxd8 Raxd8 16 Rad1, but he would be struggling there too, and in a position without the slightest hope of an attack.

15...Bxe2 16 Rxe2 cxd4 17 Bf2 Nc5 18 Bc4 Rc8 19 f5 exf5 20 exf5 d5 (Diagram 19)

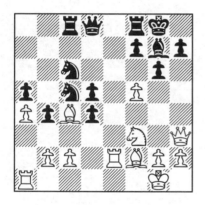

Diagram 19 (W)

Shutting out the dangerous bishop

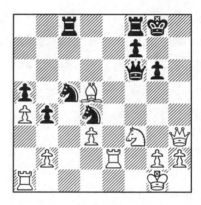

Diagram 20 (W)

White is in all sorts of trouble

Shutting the light-squared bishop out of play is Black's number one priority. Many players would be tempted by the line 20...Ne5 21 Bd5 d3 22 cxd3 Ncxd3 23 Be3 Nxf3+ 24 Qxf3 Bxb2, but after 25 Rf1 White would have strong pressure for the pawns that have gone amiss.

21 fxg6 hxg6 22 Bh4 Bf6 23 Bxf6

If 23 Bxd5 d3! (and not 23...Bxh4 24 Qxh4 Qxd5?? because of 25 Ng5) 24 Bxf6 Qxf6 25 cxd3 Nd4 would transpose back into the game.

23...Qxf6 24 Bxd5

White can defend against 24...d3 with 24 Bb5, but then 24...b3! is very strong.

24...d3 25 cxd3 Nd4 (Diagram 20)

Suddenly White is in all sorts of trouble: Black's knights are hopping in all over the show.

26 Re3

Other moves are no better; for example:

a) 26 Bxf7+ Kg7! (not 26...Kxf7?? 27 Ng5+ Qxg5 28 Qh7+ Kf6 29 Qe7+ Kf5 30 Re5+ Kg4 31 Qxg5 mate) 27 Nxd4 Qxd4+ 28 Kh1 Qf6 and White can't move the bishop away from f7 because of the mate on f1.

b) 26 Rf2 Nxd3 27 Rd2 Rcd8 28 Rxd3 Ne2+ followed by 29...Nf4 wins the exchange.

c) 26 Rd2 Ncb3 also wins the exchange.

26...Nc2 27 Re5

Or if 27 Ng5 Qxg5 28 Bxf7+ Rxf7 29 Qxc8+, then 29...Rf8 30 Re8 Qe3+ puts an end to White's fun.

27...Nxd3 0-1

White has far too many pieces en prise.

Game 23
☐ O.Sabitov ■ T.V.Petrosian
USSR Spartakiad, Moscow 1983

1 e4 d6 2 d4 g6

The great Tigran often played the Modern when he wanted to win with Black.

3 Nc3 Bg7 4 Bc4 e6

Here, too, this is an excellent move, notwithstanding the fact that White can now try plans in which he pushes his f-pawn. In the game Gausel-Davies in the introductory chapter I played 4...Nc6, but this can transpose into a Pirc after 5 Nf3 Nf6, which makes it less economical as a repertoire choice.

5 Nf3 Ne7 6 Bg5 h6 7 Bh4 a6 8 0-0 Nd7 9 Qe2 g5 (Diagram 21)

Black gains space on the kingside whilst avoiding any opening of the position like the plague.

10 Bg3 Ng6

I don't like 10...g4?! 11 Ne1 Bxd4 because after 12 Qxg4 the disappearance of two pawns would represent an opening of the position. In the game White manages to force things open, but Petrosian makes him pay for the privilege.

11 e5?!

Attempting to cut the Gordian knot by offering a pawn, but Black has everything under control.

11...g4 12 Nd2 dxe5 13 d5

13 Qxg4? would be met by 13...exd4 14 Nce4 h5, when White's pieces get driven back in confusion.

13...exd5 14 Nxd5 0-0 15 f3

And here 15 Qxg4? is strongly met by 15...Nb6, the line 16 Qxg6 fxg6 17 Nxb6+ Kh7 18 Nxa8 Qxd2 19 Nxc7 Qxc2 leaving White with inadequate compensation for his queen.

15...b5 16 Bb3 Nc5 17 Rad1 Nxb3 18 Nxb3 Qg5 19 Nd2 f5 (Diagram 22)

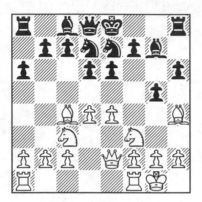

Diagram 21 (W)	**Diagram 22 (W)**
A standard hippo procedure	Rolling his pawn mass forward

White is allowed to recover his pawn by taking on c7, but this just helps Black's queen's rook get into the game.

20 Nxc7 Ra7 21 Nd5 Be6 22 f4?

Strategically this is the right idea, trying to construct a blockade on the kingside. But unfortunately for White, his dam cannot hold the huge weight of black forces.

22...Qd8 23 Nc3 Qc8

With the idea of ...b5-b4 and ...Qxc2.

24 a3 Re7 (Diagram 23) 25 Qe3?!

Losing; but even after 25 Qf2 White is in all sorts of trouble, for example 25...exf4 26 Bxf4 Nxf4 27 Qxf4 Qc5+ 28 Kh1 Be5 29 Qxh6 Rf6 30 Qg5+ Rg7 31 Qh4 Rh7 32 Qg5+ Kf7 etc.

25...exf4 26 Rxf4

26 Bxf4 Bc4 would win the exchange for starters.

26...Bd5! 27 Qf2 Nxf4 28 Bxf4 Bf7 29 Bd6 Rd7 30 Nb3

30 Bxf8 Bd4 picks up the queen.

30...Rfd8 31 Qg3 Qc6 0-1 (Diagram 24)

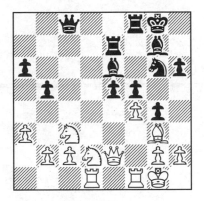

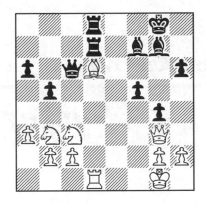

Diagram 23 (W)

White is in trouble

Diagram 24 (W)

Another piece drops off

A classic demolition job by the former World Champion. The early stages give the impression of a gerbil attempting to savage one very large cat.

Summary

Whenever White's bishop comes to c4 Black must be extremely careful about threats against f7. When he does show such caution, with the Hippoesque 4...e6, he both blunts these threats and can even look forward to harassing White's then clumsily-placed bishop. Not only can it be attacked with ...d6-d5, the flanking ...b7-b5 is also on the cards.

Chapter Five

g2-g3 Systems

Introduction

The system with g2-g3 aims at quiet harmonious development while maintaining the pawn duo on e4 and d4. Against the Pirc Defence (with ...Nf6 by Black) it has gained a reputation for being a risk-free line in which White can generate lasting positional pressure. The Modern Defence move order gives Black a more dynamic option based on counterattacking d4 with an early ...Nc6:

1 e4 g6 2 d4 Bg7 3 Nc3

The immediate 3 g3 is well met by 3...d5! **(Diagram 1)** and then:

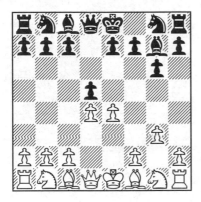

Diagram 1 (W)

A timely counterstrike

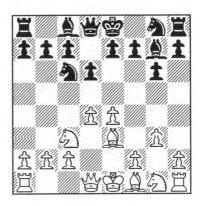

Diagram 2 (B)

Black has a pleasant choice

a) 4 exd5 Qxd5 5 Nf3 Bg4 6 Bg2 Nc6 7 c3 e5 8 h3 Bxf3 9 Bxf3 Qd7 10 0-0 exd4 11 cxd4 Nge7 12 d5 Nd4 gave Black good counterplay in N.Davies-S.Siebrecht, German League 1998.

b) 4 e5 c5 5 c3 Nc6 6 Bg2 Bf5 7 a3 Qa5 8 Ne2 cxd4 9 b4 Qa6 10 cxd4 Nxb4 won a pawn in A.Strikovic-Z.Azmaiparashvili, Candas 1992.

3...d6 4 Nge2

This is a more accurate move order than 4 g3, after which 4...Nc6 poses White quite a problem about how to defend d4. 5 Nge2 is powerfully met by 5...Bg4!, while 5 d5 Ne5 6 f4 Nd7 left White's position very exposed in Game 24, Spasov-Speelman, Biel 1993. White's best is probably 5 Be3 **(Diagram 2)**, when Black has a pleasant choice between 5...Nf6 and 5...e5.

a) 5...Nf6 may be best met by 6 h3 to stop 6...Ng4, but then 6...e5 7 dxe5 Nxe5 8 f4 Ned7 9 Bg2 0-0 10 Nge2 Qe7 11 Qd2 Nb6 12 b3 Re8 13 0-0 leads to Test Position 11 in the game J.Shaw-C.McNab, St Andrews 1993.

b) 5...e5 6 dxe5 Nxe5 7 f4 Bg4 8 Qd2 reaches Test Position 12, and even after the superior 7 h3 Black gets a comfortable game following ...Nf6 and castling. The most logical move for White is 6 Nge2, after which 6...Nf6 (threatening 7...Ng4) 7 h3 transposes to the main line (see the note with 7 g3 below).

4...Nc6 (Diagram 3)

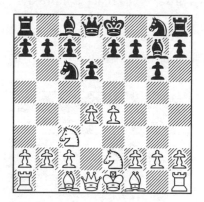

Diagram 3 (W)	**Diagram 4 (W)**
My favourite prescription	The h8-a1 diagonal is open

This is my favourite prescription, hitting d4 again.

4...a6 is also interesting here, for example 5 g3 (5 a4 Nc6 would be similar to the main line) 5...b5 6 Bg2 Bb7 7 0-0 Nd7 8 a3 c5 9 Re1 Rb8 10 Be3 cxd4 11 Bxd4 Ngf6 12 h3 0-0 was fine for Black in Y.Zilberman-N.Davies, Rishon LeZion 1994.

5 Be3

Some Whites have tried to take the initiative at this point with 5 d5, but the surrender of the e5-square and the opening of the h8-a1 diagonal is going to give Black counterplay. After 5...Ne5 6 f4 Nd7 **(Diagram 4)** 7 Be3 (7 Nd4 Ngf6 8 Be2 c5 9 dxc6 bxc6 10 Nxc6 Qb6 11 e5 dxe5 12 fxe5 was D.Belfiore-M.Ginsburg, Acasusso 1991, and now 12...Bb7 13 exf6 Bxf6 would recover the piece with an excellent game for Black) 7...Ngf6 8 Ng3 0-0 9 Be2 c6 10 0-0 cxd5 11 exd5 Nc5 12 f5 Qc7 13 Qd2 Bd7 14 a3 Na4 15 Nxa4 Bxa4, Black had counterplay in Klinger-Davies, Budapest 1988 (Game 25).

Remember, the problem with advancing pawns forward is that you can't move them back again! And you really have to believe in this to play the Modern well.

5...Nf6

Jon Speelman has preferred the unusual 5...e5 6 h3 Nge7!?, for example 7 dxe5 Nxe5 8 Nd4 0-0 9 Be2 d5 10 exd5 Nxd5 11 Nxd5 Qxd5 12 0-0 Nc4 13 Bxc4 Qxc4 was better for Black because of his bishop pair in C.Barry-J.Speelman, Dublin

1993. I haven't tried this myself because after 7 d5 the knight would have to go back to b8, but probably this is quite playable.

6 h3 e5 (Diagram 5)

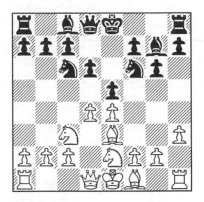

Diagram 5 (W)

Reverting to a Pirc centre

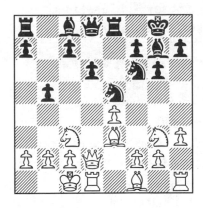

Diagram 6 (W)

A line-opening pawn sacrifice

7 dxe5

7 g3 is the logical alternative, when Black can exploit White's loss of time by hitting out in the centre with 7...d5!?. In practice I tend not to like this very much because it can lead to simplification and a rather sterile game after 8 dxe5. Instead, Black can keep the position more rich with 7...0-0 followed by a fianchetto of his queen's bishop.

7...Nxe5 8 Ng3

Now White never achieves his fianchetto. Obviously 8 g3?? Nf3 mate would not be a good idea!

8...0-0

8...Be6 9 Qd2 Nc4 is not bad either, though probably without as many dynamic chances as the text.

9 Qd2 Re8 10 0-0-0 b5!? (Diagram 6)

Offering a pawn to open lines against White's king. We are following Godena-Davies, Budapest 1993, a game which helped me gain my second Grandmaster norm (see Game 26).

Illustrative Games

Game 24
□ **V.Spasov** ■ **J.Speelman**
Biel Interzonal 1993

---

1 e4 g6 2 d4 Bg7 3 Nc3 d6 4 g3

In view of Black's reply this is quite a risky move. 4 Nge2 is a more solid way to introduce the fianchetto line.

4...Nc6 5 d5

5 Be3 is probably White's best move here.

5...Ne5 6 f4 Nd7 7 Bg2

White's pawn advances have taken some space, but have left his position very exposed in the process.

7...c6 (Diagram 7)

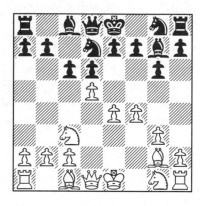

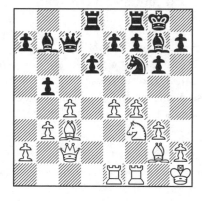

Diagram 7 (W)

The white pawns are a target

Diagram 8 (W)

Undermining the c-file

---

8 Nf3 cxd5 9 Nxd5 Nb6 10 0-0 Nxd5 11 Qxd5 Qb6+ 12 Kh1 Nf6 13 Qd3 0-0

Black has obtained a very comfortable Sicilian type structure in which the exchange of a minor piece eases his game.

14 Be3 Qc7 15 Bd4 Bd7 16 c4 Bc6 17 Rae1 Rad8 18 Bc3

And not 18 Bxa7? because of 18...b6 19 Nd4 Be8 etc.

18...b6 19 Qc2 Bb7 20 b3 b5! (Diagram 8) 21 e5

After 21 cxb5 there would follow 21...Nxe4 22 Rxe4 Bxe4 (and not 22...Bxc3?? because of 23 Rc4) 23 Qxe4 Bxc3 24 Rc1 Qa5 when White has no compensation for the exchange.

21...dxe5 22 fxe5?

With hindsight it would have been better to play 22 Nxe5, despite the weakening of White's king caused by the exchange of light-squared bishops. After 22...Bxg2+ 23 Qxg2 Nd7 24 Nxd7 Bxc3 25 Nxf8 Bxe1 26 Rxe1 bxc4 27 Nxh7 Kxh7 28 bxc4 Qxc4 Black is for preference, but with just major pieces left the smart money should be on a draw.

22...Nd5!

White may have missed this.

23 Bd2

23 cxd5 is answered by 23...b4, regaining the piece with advantage.

23...bxc4 24 Qxc4 Qxc4 25 bxc4 Nb6 (Diagram 9)

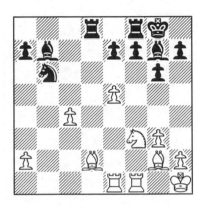

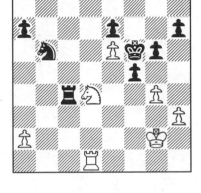

Diagram 9 (W)	**Diagram 10 (W)**
A favourable endgame for Black	The end is nigh

So Black enters an endgame with the better pawn structure, though White has some compensating space and piece activity for the time being. This calls for careful play on Black's part.

26 Bb4 Rfe8 27 e6 f5 28 Nd2 Bxg2+ 29 Kxg2 Bh6 30 Rd1 Rd4

White can no longer defend his c4-pawn.

31 Nb3 Rxc4 32 Bc5 Bg5 33 Rd4

Perhaps 33 Bd4 would have been stronger, but it's good for Black in any case.

33...Rxc5! 34 Nxc5 Be3 35 Nb3 Bxd4 36 Nxd4 Rc8 37 h3 Rc4 38 Rd1 Kg7 39 g4 Kf6

(Diagram 10)

This is a great square for the king: he attacks e6 whilst being shielded from checks along the f-file.

40 Rd3 Nd5 41 Kg3 Nc7 0-1

Game 25
☐ **J.Klinger** ■ **N.Davies**
Budapest 1988

---

1 e4 d6 2 d4 g6 3 Nc3 Bg7 4 Nge2 Nc6 5 d5 Ne5 6 f4 Nd7 7 Be3 Ngf6 8 Ng3

Another possibility is 8 h3, for example 8...c6 9 Qd2 cxd5 10 exd5 Nc5 11 g4 h5 12 g5 Nfe4 13 Nxe4 Nxe4 14 Qb4 Nc5 15 Bd4 Bxd4 16 Nxd4 0-0 gave rise to double-edged play in R.Djurhuus-M.Krasenkow, Malmo 1995.

8...0-0 9 Be2 c6 (Diagram 11)

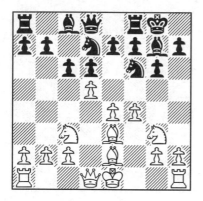
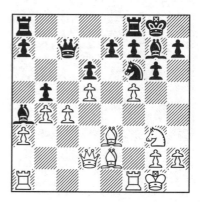

Diagram 11 (W)	Diagram 12 (W)
Challenging the centre	Undermining the d5-pawn

Attacking the advanced pawns and preparing to develop the queen.

10 0-0 cxd5 11 exd5 Nc5 12 f5 Qa5

Black can also consider simply 12...Bd7 followed by ...Rc8. In the game I have to lose time with the queen, though I do get White to commit himself on the queen-side.

13 Qd2 Bd7 14 a3 Na4 15 b4 Qc7 16 Nxa4 Bxa4 17 c4 b5! (Diagram 12)

This is essential before White consolidates with 18 Rac1. Black undermines the d5-pawn, which can't be protected by a rook on d1 because of Black's bishop on a4.

18 fxg6 fxg6

It's unusual to capture away from the centre, but I was worried about being mated on the h-file if I took with the h-pawn.

19 c5

White could try 19 Rac1, but then Black can get counterplay with 19...bxc4 20 Bxc4 Qd7 21 Bd4 Bb5. White's d5-pawn is always going to be weak.

19...dxc5 20 bxc5

And here 20 Bxc5 might have been better, meeting 20...Rad8 with 21 Rae1.

20...Rad8 21 Bf3 Bb3 22 d6 exd6 23 Qb4 Bc4 24 cxd6 Rxd6 25 Bc5 Rdd8 26 Bxf8 Bxf8

Black is going to recover the exchange but – perhaps what White missed – he can considerably improve his position before doing so. Coupled with the queenside pawn majority this spells trouble for White.

27 Qb2 Bc5+ 28 Kh1 Bd4! (Diagram 13)

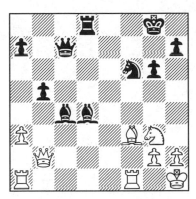

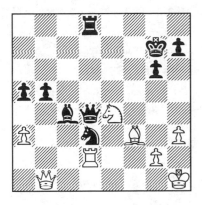

Diagram 13 (W)

Taking the other rook

Diagram 14 (W)

Forward patrol!

Much stronger than 28...Bxf1; the bishop on c4 is the anchorman for Black's position.

29 Qc2 Bxa1 30 Rxa1 Qe5 31 Rc1 Qe3 32 Qb2 Qd4 33 Qb1 Qd3 34 Qa1 Qd4

As usual aiming to gain time on the clock, rather than draw by repetition.

35 Qb1 Ng4!

If this knight is taken then g2 would become weak.

36 Ne4 Ne5 37 Rd1 Nd3 38 h3 Kg7 39 Rd2 a5 (Diagram 14) 40 Kh2 Qe5+ 41 Kg1 Qd4+ 42 Nf2

After 42 Kh2 I would probably have played 42...Re8 this time round.

42...Re8 43 Qf1 Qc5?

Overlooking a hidden drawing possibility for White. Had I seen it I would probably have chosen 43...h5, when 44 Rxd3 Bxd3 45 Qxd3 Re1+ 46 Kh2 Qxd3 47 Nxd3
Re3 wins for Black.

44 Rxd3 Bxd3 45 Qxd3 Re1+ 46 Kh2 Qxf2 47 Qc3+?

Amazingly it seems that White can actually draw here with 47 Qd7+ Kh6 (47...Kf8
48 Qd8+ Kf7 49 Qd7+ offers no respite from the checks) 48 Qd6! intending 49 Qf8+.
I don't see a way to avoid the checks, and neither does *Fritz*.

47...Kh6 48 Qc8 Qd4 49 Qf8+ Kg5 0-1

Game 26
□ **M.Godena** ■ **N.Davies**
Budapest 1993

---

1 e4 g6 2 d4 Bg7 3 Nc3 d6 4 Nge2 Nc6

It's also worth considering 4...a6 5 a4 and then 5...Nc6 (or even 5...b6). I've played
this position both ways.

5 Be3 Nf6 6 h3 e5 7 dxe5

Godena thought for quite a long time before avoiding 7 g3 d5 **(Diagram 15)** and
choosing instead a razor-sharp plan involving castling long. As I noted in the introduction, I probably wouldn't have played 7...d5 in any case because of the danger of the position becoming drawish; I play the Modern to win!

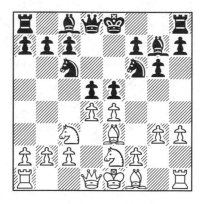

Diagram 15 (W)

A drawish continuation

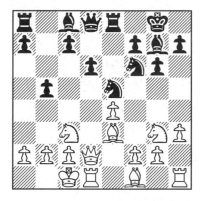

Diagram 16 (W)

A pawn for an open file!

7...Nxe5 8 Ng3 0-0

Black could equalize with 8...Be6 9 Qd2 Nc4, but I felt that the position might be rather too placid and equal for my purposes, and given that I had to win this game I was not afraid of danger. The subjectively strongest move is not always the best.

9 Qd2 Re8 10 0-0-0

When I first realized this move was coming I welcomed it because it would give me the sharp play I needed, but then I started to worry about how Black could meet ideas such as 11 f4 or 11 Bg5. Finally I decided that radical measures were called for.

 NOTE: When the two kings are castled on opposite sides, the advantage usually lies with the player who is the first to open a file.

10...b5!? (Diagram 16)

White's 11 f4 can now be met by 11...Nc4, though 11 Bg5 was still worth considering.

11 Bxb5 Bd7 12 Be2

After White's bishop retreat Black will clearly have compensation for the pawn. Godena had originally intended 12 f4!? but eventually rejected this because of the line 12...Bxb5 13 fxe5 Rxe5 14 Bd4 Qe7 15 Bxe5 Qxe5, when Black has good play for the sacrificed exchange. In the post mortem I suggested 12 Ba6, trying to inhibit Black's b-file build-up, but finally we decided that 12...Be6 would still give Black compensation for the pawn.

12...Qb8 13 f4 Nc6 14 Bf3 Qb4

Preparing to move a rook to b8 and threaten mate on b2.

15 a3 Qb7 16 e5 Rab8 17 b3

And here Godena had intended 17 Na4, but then Black has 17...dxe5 18 fxe5 Qb5 19 exf6 Bxf6 20 b3 Rxe3 21 Qxd7 Bg5, and if 22 Kb1 then 22...Rxb3+. The text is weakening, but the position remains very complicated.

17...dxe5 18 fxe5 Rxe5 19 Nge4 Qa6

It is less effective to play this move after a preliminary exchange of knights on e4. Thus 19...Nxe4 20 Nxe4 Qa6 can by met by 21 a4, after which White's defences hold.

20 a4 (Diagram 17)

In the critical position White had insufficient clock time to find the best move. White should take this opportunity to exchange on f6 as, for the time being, Black is forced to recapture with the bishop, whereas after his next move it becomes possible to take back with the queen.

20...Na5! 21 Nxf6+ Qxf6!

The move White missed, after which Black suddenly develops a ferocious attack.

22 Bd4 Qd6!

Ouch! Only now did he see that the intended 23 Bxe5 is annihilated with 23...Qa3+ 24 Kb1 Nxb3.

23 Nb1

No better are 23 Kb1 Nxb3 or 23 Kb2 Nc4+.

23...Rxb3! (Diagram 18)

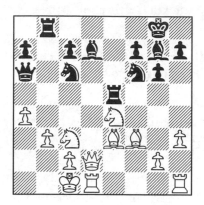

Diagram 17 (B)

The decisive mistake

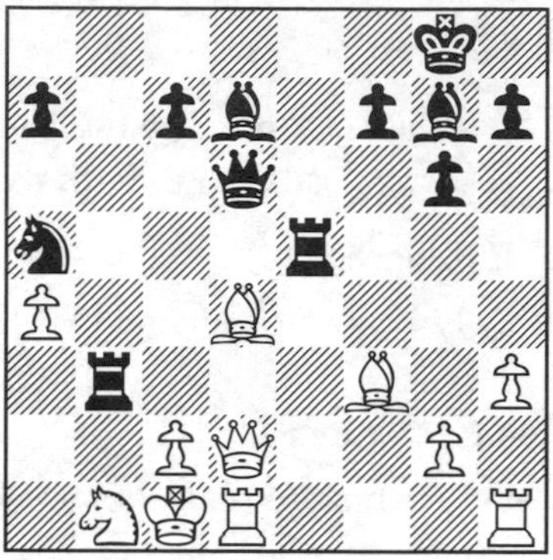

Diagram 18 (W)

Breaking through

The white king's position is imploding in dramatic fashion. By now a crowd had gathered and my opponent's flag was hanging.

24 Ba1 Qb6 0-1

White has had enough. The threat is 25...Rxb1+; the rook is immune from capture because of the knight fork picking up White's queen; while after 25 Nc3 there is either 25...Nc4 or 25...Ra3, depending on Black's mood.

Summary

The Modern Defence move order allows Black to throw a spanner in White's works at keeping a small central advantage. The counterattack with ...Nb8-c6 (either with or without a preliminary 4...a6) makes it well nigh impossible for White to continue his plan; instead he is thrown into the kind of life or death struggle in which Modern Defence players (should) thrive. White's position is not objectively bad, but it requires a certain amount of psychological adaptability. This probably explains why he often goes down in flames.

Chapter Six

The Classical 4 Nf3

- Introduction
- Illustrative Games

Introduction

The classical development of White's knights on c3 and f3 is one of the most popular ways of playing against the Modern. White hopes to keep a slight space advantage and avoid being embroiled in positions in which his centre suddenly implodes. Against this set-up I have usually chosen to transpose into a Pirc with 4...Nf6, but this gives White a wide choice of systems with 5 Be2, 5 h3, 5 Be3, 5 Bc4 and even 5 Bg5. So, instead of this, I recommend a purely 'Modern' treatment of the position with 4...a6!?.

1 e4 g6 2 d4 Bg7 3 Nc3

One of the main problems with the 4...a6 system is that White can sidestep it with 3 Nf3 d6 4 Be2. To play 4...a6 without a white knight on c3 is meaningless, and indeed White could switch to a plan based on c2-c3 and Nbd2 against this. So Black has to find a means of development in which Nf3 and Be2 costs White some options. I believe the answer lies in the move 4...Nd7 **(Diagram 1)** and then:

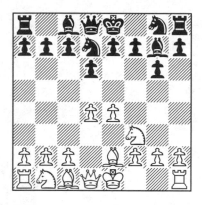

Diagram 1 (W)

Move order subtleties

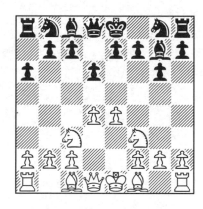

Diagram 2 (W)

Black aims for ...b7-b5

a) 5 Nc3 allows Black to transpose into the main line with 5...a6.

b) 5 c3 e5 6 0-0 Ngf6 7 Nbd2 0-0 8 Re1 Re8 9 Bf1 Nb6!? 10 h3 c6 11 a4 a5 12 Qc2 Nfd7 13 Nc4 Qc7 gave Black a solid position in Geller-Petrosian, Moscow 1981 (Game 28).

c) 5 c4 e5 6 Nc3 c6!? 7 0-0 Nh6!? is an interesting plan used in Schaufelberger-Ljubojevic, Skopje Olympiad 1972 (Game 27). Black waited for White to castle before putting his knight on h6 so as to take the sting out of a possible h2-h4.

d) 5 0-0 e5 6 Nc3 Ngf6 gives Black an improved version of the Classical Pirc, having achieved ...Nbd7 and ...e7-e5 without having to prepare this with sub-optimal moves like ...c7-c6 and ...Qc7. R.Soffer-S.Kagan, Tel Aviv 1989, continued 7 Re1 0-0 8 Bf1 Re8 9 d5?! a5 10 a3 Nc5 11 Rb1 Bd7 12 b4 axb4 13 axb4 Na4 14 Nxa4 Rxa4 15 c4 Qe7 16 Bd3 Rea8 with a nice game for Black.

3...d6 4 Nf3 a6!? (Diagram 2)

Once again this little move, aiming at a queenside expansion with ...b7-b5.

5 Be2

Besides this simple developing move White has tried a couple of others:

a) 5 Bc4 e6 6 a4 b6 7 0-0 Ne7 8 Re1 0-0 (Black could also delay this) 9 Be3 h6 10 Qd2 Kh7 11 b4 Nd7 was tense and complex in Swanson-Hillarp Persson, St Helier 2000 (Game 29).

b) 5 a4 stops Black expanding with ...b7-b5 but also rules out queenside castling for White. In Vadasz-Gorbatow, Paks 1997, Black responded with 5...b6 (5...Bg4 6 Be2 Nc6 is also playable here), after which 6 Be2 Nd7 7 0-0 Bb7 8 Re1 e6 9 Bg5 Ne7 10 h3 h6 brought about a typically complex and messy Hippopotamus position (see Game 30).

5...Nd7!

Once again an important move, in my view at least. I think that Black should play ...c7-c5 before going ...b7-b5, in order to nullify any danger in the centre.

6 0-0 c5! (Diagram 3)

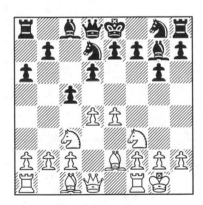
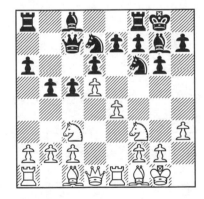

Diagram 3 (W)	Diagram 4 (W)
The most accurate move	Black has good prospects

Aiming to clarify the central tension before getting extravagant on the queenside.

 WARNING: As usual in the Modern, Black should try to break up White's pawn centre sooner rather than later.

I think that 6...b5 is very dangerous for Black after 7 e5!?, for example 7...dxe5 8 dxe5 Nxe5 9 Qxd8+ Kxd8 10 Bf4 Nd7 11 a4 bxa4 12 Rfd1 with a strong initiative; while leaving the pawn on e5 will make it difficult for Black to develop, not to mention the fact that the pawn will be a bone in his throat in the middlegame.

7 d5

Gaining space in the centre, but Black can do the same on the queenside in a way that is not normally possible in similar lines of the Schmid Benoni (1 d4 c5 2 d5 d6 3 Nc3 g6 etc). White has tried a couple of alternatives:

a) 7 Re1 cxd4 8 Nxd4 Ngf6 9 Bf1 0-0 10 Bg5 Re8 brought about a funny sort of Sicilian Dragon in Y.Fleitas-S.Siebrecht, Havana 2007. White's pieces have been developed, but not to posts which can get to grips with Black's solid Dragon pawn structure.

b) 7 Bc4!? tries to exploit the very temporary weakness of f7, but after 7...cxd4 8 Bxf7+ Kxf7 9 Ng5+ Ke8 10 Ne6 dxc3 11 Nxd8 Kxd8 Black had enough for the queen in Potkin-Kabanov, Moscow 2004 (Game 32).

7...b5 8 Re1 Ngf6

I must admit to having doctored the Doctor's move order: Nunn actually played 6...b5 and only after 7 Re1 c5 8 d5 Ngf6 reached this position.

9 Bf1 0-0 10 h3 Qc7 (Diagram 4)

We are following Britton-Nunn, London 1978. Black's space on the queenside gives him good prospects (see Game 31).

Illustrative Games

Game 27
□ **H.Schaufelberger** ■ **L.Ljubojevic**
Skopje Olympiad 1972

1 e4 g6 2 d4 Bg7 3 Nf3 d6 4 Be2

> **WARNING: Although it looks as if White is going for a Classical set-up, this move leaves open the possibility of playing either c2-c3 or c2-c4. Black needs to take account of these options, for example 4...a6?! would now be a waste of time after 5 c3!.**

4...Nd7 5 c4 e5 6 Nc3

The game reached this position via the move order 1 c4 g6 2 d4 Bg7 3 e4 d6 4 Nc3 Nd7 5 Nf3 e5 6 Be2, which is in fact an Averbakh System. Although 4...Nd7 is not the line I am recommending in Chapter Eight (instead, 4...a6!? again), at least White is committed here to a set-up with Be2 and Nf3.

6...c6

Of the other moves, 6...Ngf6 is certainly playable, but would lead to a regular King's Indian Defence. 6...Ne7 is another possibility, though the knight looks a bit passive on this square.

7 0-0 Nh6!? (Diagram 5)

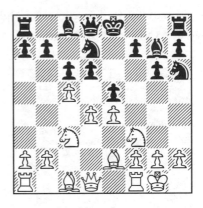

Diagram 5 (W)	**Diagram 6 (B)**
An original way to develop	Undermining Black's centre

7...Ngf6 is also playable here, but again if Black wants to play this kind of King's Indian he might as well play ...Ngf6 on the previous move.

8 d5

This certainly isn't the critical move, as Black now gets a nice Benoni position in which his f-pawn isn't blocked by a knight on f6. Indeed, the knight on h6 is very well placed since, after dropping back to f7, it will defend the weakness on d6 and prevent Nf3-g5 by White in answer to a later ...f6-f5.

Other moves are as follows:

a) 8 dxe5 dxe5 9 b3 0-0 10 Ba3 Re8 can be followed by ...f7-f6, ...Nf7 and ...Bf8 with a solid game for Black.

b) 8 Rb1 0-0 9 b4 f5 10 Bg5 (10 d5 Nf7 11 Qc2 Nf6 12 Nd2 Ng5 13 f3 fxe4 14 fxe4 cxd5 15 cxd5 Bd7 16 Qd3 Rc8 was about equal in Z.Ribli-R.Knaak, Camaguey 1974) 10...Qe8 11 d5 Nf7 12 dxc6 bxc6 13 Bc1 and now 13...Qe7 (13...Bb7 14 exf5 gxf5 15 Nh4 was unpleasant for Black in S.Reshevsky-L.Ljubojevic, Petropolis Interzonal 1973) 14 b5 fxe4 15 Nxe4 Bb7 16 Ba3 c5 looks OK for Black.

c) 8 c5!? **(Diagram 6)** 8...exd4! (8...dxc5 9 dxe5 0-0 leaves Black struggling after 10 h3, just stopping ...Nh6-g4) 9 Bxh6 Bxh6 10 Qxd4 0-0 11 cxd6 (11 Qxd6?! Qa5 gives Black counterplay because of his bishops) and now 11...Qb6! (11...Bg7?! 12 Qd2

Nc5 was played in I.Stohl-A.Berezovics, Mlada Boleslav 1993, which would have been very good for White after 13 e5!? Nd7 14 Rad1) 12 Rfd1 (or 12 Qxb6 axb6 13 Rfd1 Bg7 14 a3 b5 with compensation for the pawn in the endgame) 12...Qxb2!? 13 Nd5 Qxd4 14 Ne7+ Kh8 15 Nxd4 Nc5 and again Black has counterplay for the pawn.

8...c5 9 Rb1 0-0 10 Bd2 f6

The immediate 10...f5?! allows 11 Ng5.

11 Ne1 f5 12 Nd3 Nb6! (Diagram 7)

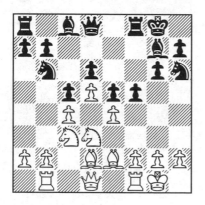

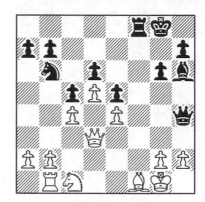

Diagram 7 (W)

Black is dong fine

Diagram 8 (W)

Coming in on the dark squares

13 Nc1?

After this retrograde move Black takes the initiative. White should probably try 13 b4!?, though Black is doing fine after 13...cxb4 (13...Nxc4 14 bxc5 is good for White) 14 Nxb4 fxe4 15 Nxe4 Bf5 16 f3 Rc8.

13...fxe4 14 Nxe4 Bf5 15 f3

15 Qc2 would have been better, when 15...Qh4 16 f3 Bxe4 can be answered by 17 Qxe4.

15...Bxe4! 16 fxe4 Qh4 17 Bxh6

White has a problem about how to defend e4. 17 Bf3? would drop the c4-pawn; 17 Qc2 loses to 17...Rxf1+ 18 Bxf1 (or 18 Kxf1 Qxh2) 18...Ng4; while after 17 Bd3 Black has 17...Nxc4! (but not 17...Ng4 18 h3 Rxf1+ 19 Qxf1 Rf8 20 Qe2 Rf2? 21 Be1!) 18 Bxc4 Qxe4, for example 19 Bd3 Qd4+ 20 Kh1 Ng4 21 Bc3 Nf2+ 22 Rxf2 Qxf2 with a rook and two pawns for the two minor pieces.

17...Bxh6 18 Qd3 Rxf1+ 19 Bxf1 Rf8 (Diagram 8) 20 Nb3?

The losing move. Instead 20 Qe2? is answered simply by 20...Nxc4; and 20 g3?

would also be bad because of 20...Rxf1+ 21 Kxf1 (if 21 Qxf1 Be3+ 22 Kg2 Qxe4+ wins the rook on b1) 21...Qxh2 when the attack is too strong; but 20 Ne2! would just about have kept White on the board.

20...Qf2+ 21 Kh1 Na4 22 Qe2 b6 0-1

There's nothing White can do about the threat of ...Na4xb2, though one gets the impression that he was probably relieved to resign.

Game 28
□ **E.Geller** ■ **T.V.Petrosian**
Moscow 1981

---

1 e4 g6 2 d4 Bg7 3 Nf3 d6 4 Be2 Nd7 5 0-0 e5 6 c3 (Diagram 9)

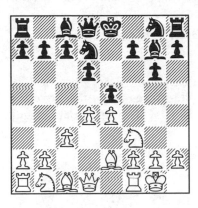

Diagram 9 (B)	Diagram 10 (W)
Geller's patented system	Preparing for d4xe5

This is Geller's patented system, relying on simple development and the maintenance of his pawn duo on e4 and d4. We shall be seeing more of this plan in the section on c2-c3 systems, in which I recommend Black plays ...Nb8-c6. Here it's OK to put the knight on d7 because of White's quiet placement of his bishop on e2.

6...Ngf6 7 Nbd2 0-0 8 Re1

Clarifying the central tension with 8 dxe5 doesn't give White much. S.Tatai-B.Ivkov, Venice 1969, went 8...dxe5 9 Re1 b6 (9...Re8 10 Bf1 Nb6 is another way to play it, getting ready to exchange White's knight should it land on c4) 10 Bf1 Bb7 11 Qc2 Re8 with approximate equality.

8...Re8 9 Bf1 Nb6!?

Very solid play. 9...b6 is another option, but Petrosian evidently preferred to avoid possibilities such as 10 Bb5!? or 10 a4 a5 11 Bb5.

10 h3 c6 11 a4 a5 12 Qc2 Nfd7!? (Diagram 10)

12...Qc7 might be a tiny bit better for White after 13 dxe5 dxe5 14 Nc4 Nxc4 15 Bxc4 Be6 16 Bxe6 Rxe6 17 Be3.

13 Nc4

The point behind Black's last move is that 13 dxe5 dxe5 14 Nc4 can now be met by 14...Nxc4 15 Bxc4 Nc5 16 Be3 Be6 with equality.

13...Qc7 14 Be3

14 dxe5 Nxc4 15 Bxc4 Nxe5 is again equal.

14...exd4 15 Bxd4

Black can meet 15 cxd4 with 15...d5, for example 16 Nxb6 Nxb6 17 e5 and now 17...Bf5 or 17...f6.

15...Nxc4 16 Bxc4 Ne5 17 Nxe5 Bxe5 18 Rad1 Bxd4 19 cxd4

19 Rxd4 is answered by 19...d5, exploiting the pin on the e-file.

19...Be6 20 Qc3?!

After this Petrosian gains a small advantage and tortures Geller for the rest of the game. White should have exchanged bishops on e6, with approximate equality.

20...Bxc4 21 Qxc4 Rxe4! (Diagram 11)

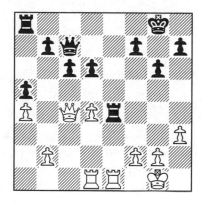

Diagram 11 (W)

A neat tactic

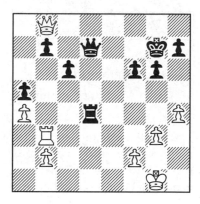

Diagram 12 (B)

What now for Black?

This neat tactic gives Black the better pawn structure

22 Rxe4 d5 23 Qd3 dxe4 24 Qxe4 Rd8 25 Rd3

25 d5 would drop the pawn after 25...Qd6.

25...Rd5

Intending 26...Qd6 followed by 27...c5. White needs to do something.

26 Rb3 Kg7 27 g3 Qd7 28 h4 f6 29 Qf4?

29 Qe1, eyeing the a5-pawn, looks a better defence.

29...Rxd4 30 Qb8 (Diagram 12)

Not 30 Rxb7? because of 30...Rd1+.

30...Rb4?

30...b5! would have refuted White's play, as 31 axb5? loses to 31...Qh3!, while if 31 Re3 Rd1+ 32 Kh2 Rd2 is very strong.

31 Rxb4 axb4 32 a5! Kf7

After 32...c5 White can hold with 33 Qa7 Qc6 34 a6 Qxa6 35 Qxc5 etc.

33 a6 bxa6 34 Qxb4 Kg7 35 Qb6 Qd1+ 36 Kh2 Qf3 37 b4! g5 38 hxg5 fxg5 39 Kg1 Qd1+ 40 Kh2 Qc2 41 Qd4+ Kf7 42 Qd7+ ½-½

Game 29
☐ **S.Swanson** ■ **T.Hillarp Persson**
St Helier 2000

---

1 e4 g6 2 d4 Bg7 3 Nf3 d6 4 Nc3 a6 5 Bc4 e6 (Diagram 13)

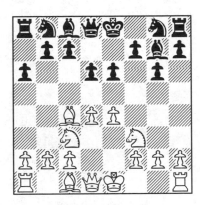

Diagram 13 (W)

The usual response to Bc4

Diagram 14 (B)

Planless play by White

As usual this is a good answer to Bf1-c4. The bishop bites on the granite pawn on e6, while Black is ready to expand on the queenside with ...b7-b5.

6 a4

For many White players this is almost a knee-jerk reaction to the 'threat' of ...b7-b5, but in doing so White makes queenside castling difficult for himself.

6...b6 7 0-0 Ne7 8 Re1 0-0

Personally speaking I don't see any reason to castle so early and Joel Benjamin evidently agrees with me. S.Solomon-J.Benjamin, Sydney 1999, went 8...Nd7 9 Bf4 Bb7 10 Qd2 h6 11 h3 g5 12 Bh2 Ng6 with a solid and flexible game. The concept of ...g6-g5 and ...Ne7-g6 is one we've come across several times already.

9 Be3 h6 10 Qd2 Kh7 11 b4?! (Diagram 14)

This has a look of frustration about it. White takes space on the queenside but not in a way that lends harmony to his position. Instead, with Black having castled so early, there's a case for 11 h4. M.Novkovic-N.Sommerbauer, Austrian League 2006, continued 11...Nd7 12 Bd3 Nf6 13 e5 Ng4 14 Bf4 dxe5 15 dxe5 Bb7 16 Qe2 Nf5 17 g3 Kg8 18 Rad1 Qe7 19 Be4 Bxe4 20 Nxe4 Qb4 21 b3 with what looks like a tiny edge for White.

11...Nd7 12 h3 Bb7 13 b5 axb5 14 axb5 Nf6 15 e5

More frustration, driving Black's knight from f6 but further exposing White's position. 15 Bd3 d5 16 exd5 Nexd5 17 Nxd5 Nxd5 would be fine for Black who can take the bishop on e3.

15...Nd7 16 exd6 cxd6 17 Be2 Nf5 18 Bf4? (Diagram 15)

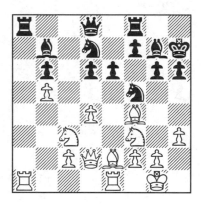

Diagram 15 (B)

White drops a pawn

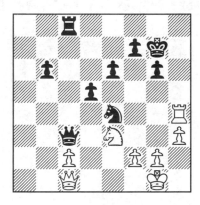

Diagram 16 (W)

Black is winning

A blunder, leaving the d4-pawn loose. Almost anything would have been better.

18...Rxa1 19 Rxa1 Bxf3 20 Bxf3 Nxd4 21 Bc6

And not 21 Bxd6? because of 21...Ne5 22 Bxe5 Nxf3+ followed by 23...Qxd2.

21...Qc7 22 Bxh6

After 22 Bxd7 Qxd7 23 Bxh6 Bxh6 24 Qxd4, Black wins a pawn with 24...Bg7 25 Qd3 Bxc3 26 Qxc3 Qxb5 etc.

22...Nxc6 23 Bxg7 Kxg7 24 bxc6 Qxc6 25 Nd1 Rc8 26 Ne3 Nf6 27 Rb1 Qc5

27...d5 is also good.

28 Rb4 d5 29 Rh4 Ne4 30 Qc1 Qc3 (Diagram 16) 31 Ng4 g5 32 Rh5 f6 33 f3 Ra8 0-1

Game 30
□ **L.Vadasz** ■ **A.Gorbatow**
Paks 1997

---

1 Nf3 d6 2 d4 g6 3 e4 Bg7 4 Nc3 a6 5 a4

This almost seems like a defensive move already. White stops the 'threat' of ...b7-b5 but takes away his own option of castling long.

5...b6

Black has another good move here in 5...Bg4, when 6 Be3 Nc6 7 Be2 (note that the inclusion of ...a7-a6 and a2-a4 means that White doesn't have Bf1-b5 available, which would be a good option had Black played 4...Bg4 5 Be3 Nc6) 7...e5 8 dxe5 dxe5 9 0-0 Nge7 10 Nd5 Nxd5 11 exd5 Ne7 12 c4 0-0 13 h3 Bxf3 14 Bxf3 Nf5 15 Bc5 Re8 was about equal in R.Elseth-N.Davies, Hamar 1983.

6 Be2 Nd7 7 0-0 Bb7 8 Re1 e6 (Diagram 17)

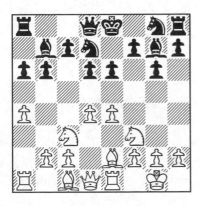
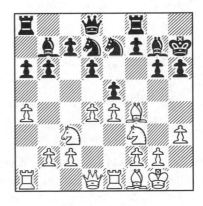

Diagram 17 (W)
Our friend the Hippopotamus

Diagram 18 (W)
Equalizing in the centre

It's never easy for White to get to grips with this mud dwelling beast, especially for weaker players – and here we see an experienced Hungarian GM floundering.

9 Bg5

If anything this is already helpful to Black because he wants to play both ...Ne7 and ...h7-h6 anyway.

9...Ne7 10 h3 h6 11 Be3 0-0

This is not forced by any means. 11...g5 followed by 12...Ng6 is a familiar alternative, leaving the king where it is for the time being. White isn't going to be opening the centre in a hurry.

12 Bf1 Kh7 13 Bf4 e5! (Diagram 18)

Equalizing in the centre.

14 dxe5 dxe5 15 Bg3 f6

With e5 solidly protected and White's bishop out of play on g3, Black certainly has nothing to fear. If anything it is White who must now play carefully not to fall behind.

16 Nd2 Nc5 17 Nc4 Qe8 18 f3 Rd8 19 Qc1 h5 20 Bf2 Ne6 (Diagram 19)

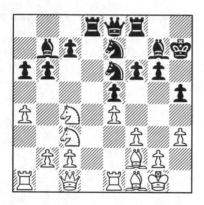

Diagram 19 (W)

Targeting the d4-square

Diagram 20 (W)

This should be drawn

Black targets the d4-square. This often happens in Pirc/Modern positions, the culprit being White's 3 Nc3, making it difficult to cover d4 with a pawn! Am I joking? No, not altogether.

21 Nb1 Nd4 22 Nbd2 Bh6 23 Be3 Bxe3+ 24 Nxe3 a5 25 c3 Ne6 26 Bb5 Bc6 27 Bxc6 Qxc6 28 Ndf1

This is a bit retrograde. 28 Qc2 looks like a better move.

28...Nf4 29 Qc2 Qc5 30 Rad1 h4 31 Rxd8 Rxd8 32 Rd1 Rd6 33 Rxd6 Qxd6 (Diagram 20)

34 Qf2 g5 35 Qd2 Nc8 36 Nf5 Qd3 37 Qxd3?

It looks as if time trouble might have been a factor here, as this just loses a pawn. Both 37 Qe1 and 37 Kh2 look playable.

37...Nxd3 38 b3 Nc1 39 Nd2 Ne2+ 40 Kf2 Nxc3 0-1

Game 31
□ **R.Britton** ■ **J.Nunn**
London 1978

---

1 e4 g6 2 d4 Bg7 3 Nc3 d6 4 Nf3 a6 5 Be2 Nd7 6 0-0 c5 (Diagram 21)

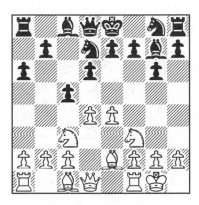
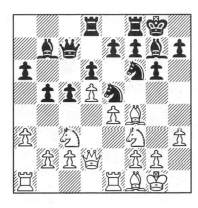

Diagram 21 (W)
The accurate move order

Diagram 22 (W)
Not fearing doubled pawn

The actual move order was 6...b5 7 Re1 c5 8 d5, but the problem then is that White can throw a spanner in the works with 7 e5, as described in the introduction to this chapter.

7 Re1 b5

A good alternative for Black is just 7...cxd4 8 Nxd4 Ngf6, reaching an unusual sort of Sicilian Dragon in which White has castled kingside. This is very comfortable for Black, for example 9 Bf1 0-0 10 Bg5 Re8 11 Qd2 Nc5 12 Rad1 b5 13 b4?! Ncd7 14 Nd5 Bb7 15 Nb3 Rc8 16 Na5 Bxd5 17 exd5 Nb6 and in Y.Fleitas-S.Siebrecht, Havana 2007, Black had the better game because of White's weaknesses along the c-file. White's 13 b4 was a weird and wild idea.

8 d5 Ngf6 9 Bf1 0-0 10 h3 Qc7 11 a3 Bb7 12 Bf4 Rad8 13 Qd2 Ne5! (Diagram 22) 14 Qe3

White can give Black doubled e-pawns with 14 Nxe5 dxe5, when 15 Bg5 e6 16 Qe3 reaches the same position as in the next note.

14...e6 15 Bxe5

15 Nxe5 dxe5 16 Bg5 would have been a better idea, which Black should probably meet with 16...exd5 17 exd5 Qc8, for example 18 a4 b4 19 Ne4 Nxd5 20 Qxc5 f6 21 Bh4 Rd7 intending ...Rfd8 and an advance of his kingside pawns (...g6-g5 and ...f6-f5). My own preference would be for Black's position.

15...dxe5 16 dxe6 fxe6

Black has contracted doubled and isolated pawns on the e-file, but he has two bishops as compensation and the pawns cover a lot of squares. Nunn's forthcoming exchange sacrifice unleashes the power of the bishops, making this a very attractive game.

17 Nd2 Rd4! 18 f3 Nh5 19 Ne2 Nf4! (Diagram 23)

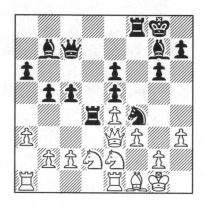

Diagram 23 (W)

A beautifully thematic move

Diagram 24 (W)

Black wins

20 Nxd4 exd4 21 Qf2 Be5 22 a4?

22 g3 Nh5 23 f4 is an attempt to cover the weak dark squares, but then Black could make it a whole rook with 23...Nxg3 (23...g5!? is also possible) 24 Qxg3 Bxf4, when it's not easy to find a move for White; for example 25 Qg2 Be3+ 26 Rxe3 dxe3 27 Nf3 Bxe4 28 Be2 Bxc2 gets a lot of pawns for the piece, or if 25 Qd3 c4 26 Nxc4 bxc4 27 Qxc4 Qe5 with a very strong attack.

22...Nh5 23 g4 Bg3 24 Qe2 Nf4 25 Qd1 c4

Disdaining the miserable rook on e1.

26 axb5 axb5 27 Bg2 Bxe1 28 Qxe1 e5 29 Nf1 Qc5 30 Kh2 d3 31 cxd3 Nxd3 32 Qd2 Qd4 33 Rb1? Bxe4! (Diagram 24) 34 fxe4 Rf2 35 Qg5 Rxg2+! 36 Kxg2 Nf4+ 0-1

After 37 Kf3 Qd3+ it's a forced mate.

Game 32
□ **V.Potkin** ■ **N.Kabanov**
Moscow 2004

1 e4 g6 2 d4 Bg7 3 Nc3 a6 4 Nf3 d6 5 Be2 Nd7 6 0-0 c5 7 Bc4!? (Diagram 25)

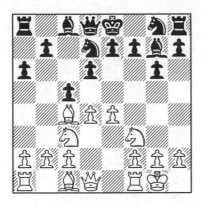

Diagram 25 (B)

An aggressive attempt

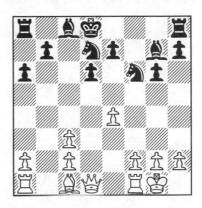

Diagram 26 (W)

Three pieces for the queen

An aggressive attempt to take advantage of Black's 6...c5. A similarly motivated idea is 7 dxc5 Nxc5 8 e5!?, but this seems to be fine for Black after 8...Bf5, for example 9 Be3 Rc8 10 exd6 Bxc3! 11 bxc3 Qxd6 12 Qxd6 exd6 13 Rfe1 Ne7 with Black's superior pawn structure balancing White's bishop pair.

7...cxd4

7...e6 looks like a solid alternative, for example 8 Bg5 Ne7 9 dxc5 Nxc5 10 e5 d5 11 Qd4 Qc7 with equality.

8 Bxf7+ Kxf7 9 Ng5+ Ke8 10 Ne6 dxc3 11 Nxd8 Kxd8 12 bxc3 Ngf6 (Diagram 26)

So Black gets three minor pieces for his queen, but king safety and their ability to coordinate are vital factors here.

13 Re1 Rf8?!

I don't think this is right. The number one priority for Black is to prevent things opening up after e4-e5. With this in mind I like 13...Ne8!, for example 14 Qd2 b6 15 f4 Bb7 16 e5 Rc8, keeping the position closed while Black completes his development.

14 f4 a5

Developing the rook on a6 looks clumsy but Black needs to get it out somewhere and defend d6. After a sensible-looking move like 14...Nc5, White gets a dangerous attack with 15 e5 Nfe4 16 exd6 exd6 17 Ba3.

15 e5 Ne8 16 Ba3 Ra6 17 Qd2 Rc6 18 c4! b6?

For better or worse 18...Rxc4 was the only show in town. After 19 Rad1 Rfxf4 20 exd6 Nxd6 21 Bxd6 exd6 22 Qxd6 Bd4+ 23 Kh1 Bc5 Black manages to cobble together a defence.

19 Rad1 Rxc4 20 exd6 exd6 (Diagram 27)

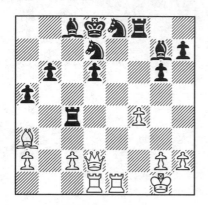

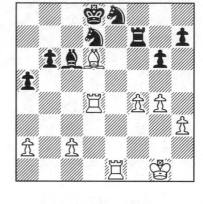

Diagram 27 (W)	Diagram 28 (W)
White can win	Heading for a draw

21 Bxd6?

Missing a win with 21 Qd5!, for example 21...Rfxf4 22 Rxe8+ Kxe8 23 Qe6+ Kd8 24 Bxd6 Rfe4 25 Qg8+ etc.

21...Bd4+ 22 Qxd4 Rxd4 23 Rxd4?

Here 23 Be7+ Kc7 24 Rxd4 is the right way, which is probably about equal after 24...Rf7.

23...Rf7?

Now 23...Nxd6 24 Rxd6 Rxf4 is good for Black.

24 g4?

24 Ba3 is better. It seems likely that time trouble was already a factor in this game.

24...Bb7?

24...Nxd6 25 Rxd6 Rxf4 is just as good as on the previous move.

25 h3 Bc6 (Diagram 28)

25...Nxd6 26 Rxd6 Rxf4 is less clear now because of 27 Red1 Rf7 28 Rxb6. From here on things appear to calm down a bit, with the remainder of the game looking relatively solid.

26 Kh2 Nc7 27 Kg3 Kc8 28 c4 Na6 29 Kh4 Nac5 30 Kg5 Ba4 31 Rd2 Bc6 32 Rd4 Ba4 33 Rd2 ½-½

Summary

When White is more modest with his pawn advances it becomes harder to rip him limb from limb. Even so Black can spike the play with the ubiquitous 4...a6, aiming for a queenside expansion with ...b7-b5.

The flexible 4 Be2 aims to transpose to a Classical Pirc after 4...Nf6, but Black has a good way to avoid it in 4...Nd7. This can lead to slightly different treatments of the Geller System (with c2-c3) and the Averbakh (with c2-c4) to the ones I am suggesting in the next chapters, but White has also committed his bishop to e2 rather earlier than might like in those lines.

Chapter Seven

Early c2-c3 Systems

Introduction

In this chapter I will examine some set-ups for White which are hardly dealt with by the books but tend to occur very frequently in practice. They all involve rather innocuous-looking moves which are aimed at strengthening White's position rather than trying to take a lot of space or launching an early attack.

1 e4 g6 2 d4 Bg7 3 c3 d6

I've often played 3...Nf6 **(Diagram 1)**

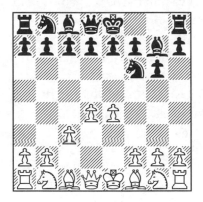

Diagram 1 (W)

Playing in Alekhine style

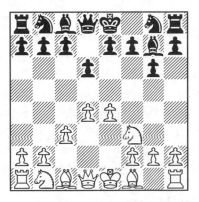

Diagram 2 (B)

A quiet but solid set-up

4 e5 Nd5 in this position, the idea of which is that 3 c3 will be a lost tempo for White if he now opts for 5 c4. So instead of 5 c4 White should probably play 5 f4, when 5...d6 6 Nf3 dxe5 7 fxe5 0-0 8 Bc4 c5 9 dxc5 Be6 10 Qd4 Nc6 11 Qe4 Na5 gave Black very interesting counterplay in a game L.Ljubojevic-J.Timman, Malaga 1971.

In answer to 3...Nf6 most of my opponents have played 4 Bd3, after which 4...0-0 once again delays ...d7-d6. If White now plays 5 f4 Black can continue with 5...d5 6 e5 Ne4, when 7 Nd2 f5 cements the position of the knight on e4. P.Holian-N.Davies, Liverpool League 1981, continued 8 Ngf3 b6 9 0-0 c6 10 Qe1 Ba6 11 Bxa6 Nxa6 12 Nxe4 dxe4 13 Nd2 Nc7 with an excellent game for Black.

4 Nf3 (Diagram 2)

White hopes to neutralize the g7-bishop and keep a small advantage in the centre. There are several other possibilities:

a) 4 Bd3 Nc6 5 Ne2 was played against me in G.Waddingham-N.Davies, British Championship, Southport 1983. The game went 5...e5 6 dxe5 Nxe5 7 Bc2 Nf6 8 Bg5 h6 9 Bh4 g5 10 Bg3 Nh5 11 Bb3 Qf6 12 Na3 Nf4 13 Bxf4 gxf4 14 Nd4 Qg5 and Black had the initiative.

b) 4 Bg5 Nf6 5 Nd2 continues White's harmonious mobilization. In this position I have usually gone for ...Nb8-c6 plans, for example 5...Nc6 (or 5...h6 6 Bh4 Nc6 7 Ngf3 g5 8 Bg3 Nh5 9 Bc4 e6 as in Game 34, Gil-Davies, Linares 1987) 6 Bd3 h6 7 Bh4 e5 8 Ne2 g5 9 Bg3 Nh5 10 dxe5 dxe5 11 Nc4 Nf4 12 Bxf4 exf4 with the better chances because of the bishop pair in Johnsen-Davies, Gausdal 1993 (Game 33).

c) 4 f4 Nf6 5 e5 dxe5 6 fxe5 Nd5 7 Nf3 transposes to Ljubojevic-Timman in the note to Black's third move, while after 5 Bd3 I like the pawn sacrifice 5...0-0 6 Nf3 c5 7 dxc5 Nbd7! 8 cxd6 exd6, for example 9 0-0 Nc5 10 Qc2 Re8 11 Nbd2 Bd7! 12 Nd4 Rc8 13 Kh1 Qe7 14 f5 Nfxe4 15 Bxe4 Nxe4 16 fxg6 hxg6 17 Nxe4 Qxe4 18 Qb3 Be6 19 Nxe6 Rxe6 and Black's active major pieces gave him the better game in Hodgson-Norwood, British Championship 1989 (see Game 35).

4...Nf6 5 Bd3 0-0 6 0-0 Nc6 7 b4

Gaining space on the queenside and attempting to stop ...e7-e5 mechanically with the idea of b4-b5.

There is a major alternative in 7 Re1, e.g. 7...e5 8 Nbd2 Nh5 9 Nb3 and then:

a) 9...Bg4 was played in Blodstein-Belov, Voskresensk 1993 (Game 36).

b) 9...h6 10 h3 Qf6 11 Bf1 Nf4 12 Kh2 g5 13 g3 Ng6 14 Be3 Nge7 15 Nfd2 Qg6 16 Bc4 Kh8 17 g4 exd4 18 Nxd4 Nxd4 19 Bxd4 Bxd4 20 cxd4 Qf6 21 Nf3 Ng6 22 Rc1 c6 23 e5 dxe5 24 dxe5 Qf4+ 25 Kg2 Be6 26 Qc2 led to Test Position 21 (Dutreeuw-Speelman, Antwerp 1993).

7...Nh5!? (Diagram 3)

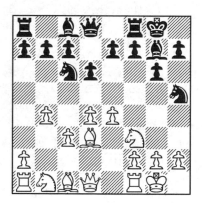

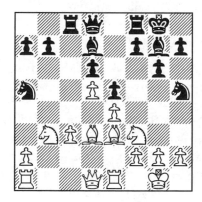

Diagram 3 (W)	**Diagram 4 (W)**
Black plans ...e7-e5	Black has an excellent game

This curious-looking knight move aims to play ...e7-e5.

An interesting alternative is 7...Bg4 as in P.Leko-Cu.Hansen, Copenhagen 1995, which continued 8 h3?! (8 Nbd2 was probably White's best, when 8...e5 9 d5 Ne7 10 h3 Bd7 11 c4 Nh5 12 Nb3 Nf4 would have led to complex play) 8...Bxf3 9 Qxf3

Nd7 10 Nd2 (10 b5? is bad because of 10...Nxd4!, winning material) 10...e5 11 d5 Ne7 12 Qe2 c6 13 c4 cxd5 14 cxd5 Nxd5! 15 exd5 e4 16 Rb1 exd3 17 Qxd3 Ne5 and White was struggling to equalize.

8 b5

After 8 Be3 Black could play 8...e5 9 d5 Ne7 10 c4 f5 with a kind of souped-up King's Indian.

8...Na5 9 Re1 c5 10 bxc6 Nxc6 11 Be3 e5 12 d5 Na5 13 Nbd2 Bd7 14 Nb3 Rc8! (Diagram 4)

Black had an excellent game in Korchnoi-Azmaiparashvili, Madrid 1996 (see Game 37).

Illustrative Games

Game 33
☐ **Sv.Johnsen** ■ **N.Davies**
Gausdal 1993

1 e4 g6 2 d4 d6 3 Bg5 Bg7 4 c3 Nf6 5 Nd2 Nc6

Black can also play 5...h6 first, as in the next game.

6 Bd3 h6 7 Bh4 e5

After the immediate 7...g5 8 Bg3, the white queen covers h5. So Black must get White to develop his king's knight before hunting down White's dark-squared bishop.

8 Ne2 g5 9 Bg3 Nh5 10 dxe5 dxe5 11 Nc4 Nf4!

Much better than 11...Nxg3 12 Nxg3, when the f5-square can be targeted by both white knights (Nc4-e3 brings the other one across). Now White has to take because both g2 and d3 are attacked.

12 Bxf4 exf4! (Diagram 5)

Opening up the long diagonal for the Modern bishop on g7. Black also accesses the e5-square and can claim to have the advantage.

> **TIP: The activity of Black's dark-squared bishop is one of the key factors in the Modern.**

13 Qc2 Be6 14 h4 Qe7 15 hxg5 hxg5 16 Rxh8+ Bxh8 17 0-0-0?! Qc5 18 Qa4 0-0-0 (Diagram 6)

Threatening both the f2-pawn and 19...Rxd3. White is already losing.

19 Nd4 Nxd4 20 cxd4 Rxd4 21 b3 b5 22 Qa6+ Kb8 23 Qa5 Qc6 24 Qb4 Kc8 25 Bc2 bxc4 26 Qf8+ Kb7 27 Qxh8 cxb3 0-1

Diagram 5 (W)

Opening up the long diagonal

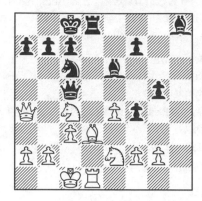

Diagram 6 (W)

White is already losing

After 28 cxb3 Bxb3 White faces a ruinous loss of material with mate to follow.

Game 34
□ **J.Gil** ■ **N.Davies**
Linares 1987

---

1 e4 d6 2 d4 g6 3 c3 Bg7 4 Bg5 Nf6 5 Nd2 h6 6 Bh4 Nc6 7 Ngf3

7 Bd3 would transpose to the previous game.

7...g5 (Diagram 7)

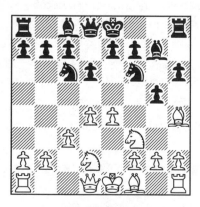

Diagram 7 (W)

Hunting the bishop down

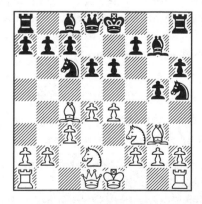

Diagram 8 (W)

Black's plan is revealed

Chasing down White's dark-squared bishop, albeit at the expense of weakening the kingside pawn structure.

8 Bg3 Nh5 9 Bc4 e6 (Diagram 8)

Black's plan is revealed. After gaining the bishop pair he intends to fortify his position and gradually catch up in development. And if the game opens up later on, his two bishops will come into their own. This explains why White now tries to attack whilst he is still ahead in development. But the drawback to his next move is that it further weakens the dark squares.

10 d5?! exd5 11 Bxd5 0-0 12 0-0 Kh8

Unpinning the f-pawn so that it can advance to f5.

13 Bxc6 bxc6 14 Nd4 Nxg3 15 fxg3

Recapturing away from the centre is 'anti-positional', but White wants to keep his pieces active.

15...Bd7 16 Qh5 (Diagram 9)

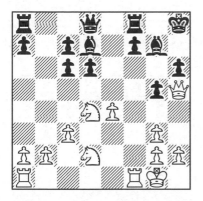

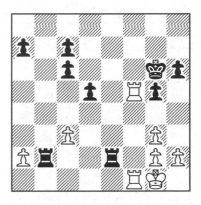

Diagram 9 (B)	Diagram 10 (W)
Black is better here	Rooks on the seventh

White's moves look expansive but he has the weaker pawn structure and faces a dangerous bishop pair. Black is better here.

16...Rb8 17 Nc4 d5

Going after the b2-pawn. White gets some initiative but it doesn't look like enough against accurate defence.

18 Ne3 Rxb2 19 e5 Qe8 20 Nef5 f6!

This offer to exchange queens breaks the attack

21 Nxg7 Kxg7 22 Nf5+ Bxf5 23 exf6+ Kg8 24 Qxe8 Rxe8 25 f7+

25 Rxf5 is not really any better; after 25...Kf7 White would have to play 26 Rf2 in order to meet the threat of 26...Ree2.

25...Kxf7 26 Rxf5+ Kg6 27 Raf1 Ree2 (Diagram 10) 28 Rf6+ Kh5 29 g4+

29 R1f2 would lead to a hopeless pawn endgame.

29...Kxg4 30 Rxh6

If 30 h3+ Kh5 31 g4+ Kh4 32 Rxh6+ Kg3 would be the end of the road for White.

30...Rxg2+ 31 Kh1 Rxa2 32 Rh7 a5 33 Rd1 a4

The a-pawn edges ever closer to the queening square.

34 h3+ Kf5 35 Rxc7 Rh2+ 36 Kg1 Rag2+ 37 Kf1 Rd2 38 Rxd2 Rxd2 39 Rxc6 a3 40 Ke1 0-1

Black wins with 40...a2 41 Ra6 Rb2 etc.

Game 35
☐ **Ju.Hodgson** ■ **D.Norwood**
British Championship, Plymouth 1989

---

1 e4 g6 2 d4 Bg7 3 c3 d6 4 f4 Nf6 5 Bd3 0-0 6 Nf3 c5 7 dxc5 Nbd7!? (Diagram 11)

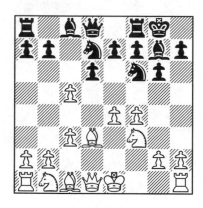
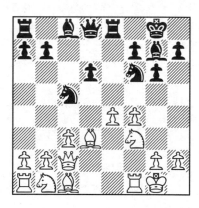

Diagram 11 (W)	**Diagram 12 (W)**
A dangerous gambit	Increasing the pressure on e4

 NOTE: This sacrifice shows the dark side of White's ambitious play. If pawns could move backwards White would want to put his f-pawn back on f2.

8 cxd6

In Y.Afek-M.Pein, Tel Aviv 1992, White's ambitious 8 b4 was strongly met by 8...a5 (8...dxc5 9 e5 Nd5 10 Be4 is what White wanted), when 9 cxd6 exd6 10 0-0 axb4 11 Bc2 Qb6+ 12 Qd4 bxc3 13 Qxb6 Nxb6 was just better for Black.

8...exd6 9 0-0

In one of the early games with this line, O.Rodriguez Vargas-R.Keene, Skopje Olympiad 1972, White played 9 Be3, after which 9...Nxe4! (rather than 9...Re8, when White should have played 10 Nbd2) 10 Bxe4 Re8 would have been best, for example 11 Qd3 (if 11 Nbd2 d5) 11...Nf6 12 Ng5 (or 12 Bxg6 hxg6 13 0-0 Bf5 14 Qd2 Ne4 with excellent play for the pawn) 12...Nxe4 13 Nxe4 Bf5 regains the piece with the better game.

9...Nc5 10 Qc2

10 e5 dxe5 11 Nxe5 Ng4 12 Bc4 Nxe5 13 fxe5 Qxd1 14 Rxd1 Be6 15 Na3 Bxe5 16 Be3 Rfc8 gave Black comfortable equality in M.Lodhi-D.Norwood, Dhaka 1993.

10...Re8 (Diagram 12) 11 Nbd2

Here, too, 11 e5 is well met by 11...dxe5 12 Nxe5 Ng4, for example 13 Bc4 Nxe5 14 fxe5 Be6 15 Bxe6 Rxe6 gave Black a nice game in A.Yastrebov-M.Pein, British League 1999.

11...Bd7!

Probably better than the 11...Nxd3 of R.Lau-Ju.Hodgson, Wijk aan Zee 1989, when after 12 Qxd3 Nxe4 13 Nxe4 Bf5 White could have played 14 Nfg5 (14 Qxd6 Rxe4 15 Qxd8+ Rxd8 soon petered out to a draw in the game) 14...d5 15 Nxf7 Kxf7 16 Ng5+ Kg8 17 Qb5 with some problems for Black.

12 Nd4

Getting ready to take Black's bishop off should it go to c6. White has also tried two other moves here:

a) 12 f5 d5! (12...Bc6 13 fxg6 hxg6 14 Nd4 Bxe4 15 Nxe4 Ncxe4 was A.Serov-I.Zakharevich, Sosnovy Bor 2002, and now 16 Bf4 would have been better for White) 13 fxg6 hxg6 14 exd5 (or 14 e5 Ng4) 14...Nxd3 15 Qxd3 Bf5 followed by ...Nxd5 gives Black excellent play for the pawn.

b) 12 Re1, as in S.Martinovic-M.Todorcevic, Timisoara 1977, is well met by 12...Qb6 (rather than Todorcevic's 12...Rc8) when 13 Nc4 Qa6! 14 e5 Nxd3 15 Qxd3 dxe5 16 fxe5 Bb5 is very good.

12...Rc8 13 Kh1

After 13 f5 Qe7 Black will win his pawn back with a good game.

13...Qe7 14 f5 Nfxe4

Perhaps it would have been better to play 14...Nxd3 15 Qxd3 Nxe4 16 fxg6 hxg6 17 Nxe4 Qxe4, the point being that in this version White can't play his queen to b3.

15 Bxe4 Nxe4 16 fxg6 hxg6 17 Nxe4 Qxe4 18 Qb3 Be6 19 Nxe6 Rxe6 20 Bf4 Rc5!? (Diagram 13)

Black's d-pawn is weak but he has active piece play as compensation.

21 Bg3 Rf5 22 Rxf5 gxf5

Preparing to set light to White's kingside with ...f5-f4-f3.

23 Qd1 Be5 24 Bxe5?!

Trying to expose Black's king, but just uniting his pawns. White should have played 24 Qf3 when the position looks balanced.

24...dxe5 25 Qd2 f4 26 Re1 Qf5 27 Qd5! b6 28 h3 Kg7 29 b4 Kg6

Getting ready for ...e5-e4.

30 Re4

On 30 Qd8 Black can go ahead with 30...e4, escaping the checks after 31 Qg8+ Kf6 32 Qh8+ Kg5 33 Qd8+ Qf6 34 Qg8+ Kh6 etc.

30...Kf6 31 c4 f3! (Diagram 14) 32 Re1?

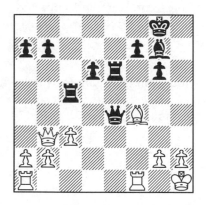

Diagram 13 (W)

Black has active piece play

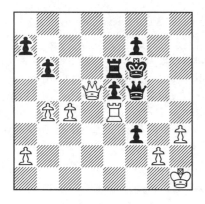

Diagram 14 (W)

White must be careful

This looks natural, but now Black's e-pawn joins the battle. White should have played 32 Kg1, after which 32...fxg2 33 Kxg2 Kg7 34 Rg4+ Rg6 35 Rxg6+ seems to be enough to draw with c4-c5 to follow.

32...e4! 33 Rf1

33 Qxf5+ Kxf5 34 gxf3 e3 would be a very unpleasant rook endgame for White, despite the fact that he is temporarily a pawn up.

33...Re5?!

Time trouble was affecting the play at this point. 33...Kg6 would have been simpler, transposing into the previous note after 34 Qxf5+ Kxf5 35 gxf3 e3.

34 Qd4 Kg6 35 Qg1 Kf6 36 Qd4 Kg7 37 c5 bxc5 38 bxc5 Kh7 39 c6 Rd5?!

Here Black should have played 39...Re6, and if 40 Qc4 Rg6 is strong.

40 Qe3??

On the last move before the time control White blunders. He had to play 40 Qf2!, when the outcome would still be up for grabs.

40...Rd3 (Diagram 15)

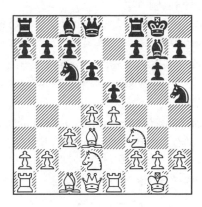

Diagram 15 (W)	**Diagram 16 (W)**
Black is winning	Putting pressure on d4 and f4

41 Qf2

Black is also winning after 41 g4 Qd5 42 Qf2 Qxc6 or just 41...Rxe3 42 gxf5 Rc3.

41...fxg2+ 42 Qxg2 Rxh3+ 43 Kg1 Qc5+ 44 Rf2 Qc1+ 45 Qf1 Qg5+ 46 Rg2

If 46 Qg2 Rg3 wins the queen.

46...Qh5 0-1

The threat of 47...Rh1+ is a killer.

Game 36
□ **A.Blodstein** ■ **I.Belov**
Voskresensk 1993

---

1 e4 d6 2 d4 g6 3 c3 Nf6 4 Bd3 Bg7 5 Nf3 0-0 6 0-0 Nc6 7 Re1

WARNING: The main problem with this line is that Black can sometimes end up in a passive position. So he should avoid routine moves and try to gain counterplay against d4. Another idea is to angle for ...f7-f5.

7...e5 8 Nbd2 Nh5 (Diagram 16)

Putting pressure on d4 and probing the f4-square.

9 Nb3 Bg4 10 Be2!

10 d5 Ne7 intending ...f7-f5 resembles a Classical King's Indian, but with White's pieces poorly placed to pursue his traditional queenside assault.

10...h6 11 h3 Bc8

If 11...Bd7, then 12 dxe5 dxe5 13 Nc5 is annoying.

12 Be3 Nf4

There's a decent alternative here in 12...Re8, putting pressure on e4. After 13 Qc2 Qf6 14 Nh2 Nf4 Black would have active play on the kingside.

13 Bf1

A double-edged position would arise after 13 Bxf4 exf4 14 Bf1 Bd7 15 Qd2 g5 16 Rad1 Qe7, with Black having the two bishops and mobile pawns on the kingside, and White a strong centre which deprives Black's pieces of some squares.

13...g5!? (Diagram 17)

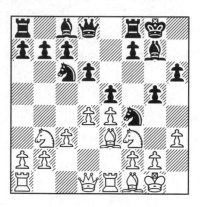

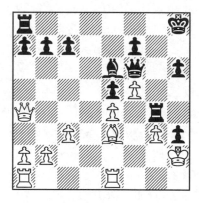

Diagram 17 (W)

Planning a later ...g5-g4

Diagram 18 (W)

Starting a spectacular attack

Supporting the knight on f4 whilst introducing the possibility of ...g5-g4.

14 dxe5

14 Kh2 f5!? also gives Black active play.

14...Nxe5 15 Nxe5

15 Bxf4 gxf4 16 Nxe5 Bxe5 17 Qh5 Qg5 is at least equal for Black.

15...Bxe5 16 Nd4 Qf6 17 Nf3 Be6 18 Nxe5 dxe5 19 Qa4 Kh8!

Getting ready to open the g-file with ...g5-g4.

20 Kh2 g4 21 g3

21 hxg4 Rg8 22 g3?! Rxg4 would give Black a very strong attack.

21...Nxh3 22 Bxh3 gxh3 23 f4 Rg8 24 f5 Rg4! (Diagram 18)

The immediate 24...Rxg3! looks even stronger: 25 Kxg3 Rg8+ 26 Kf3 (if 26 Kh2 Rg2+ 27 Kh1 Qg7 wins) 26...Rg2! (threatening ...Qh4, and better than 26...Bxf5 27 exf5 Qxf5+ 28 Bf4! Qg4+ 29 Ke3 exf4+ 30 Kd2 Qg2+ 31 Kc1 Qf2! 32 Qd4+ Qxd4 33 cxd4 Rg2 34 Rh1 h2, though Black is probably winning here too) 27 Bf4 (if 27 Re2 or 27 Rg1 then 27...Bxf5! wins) 27...Qh4 28 Bxe5+ Kh7 29 Qd4 Bc4!! **(Diagram 19)** – this amazing computer move gives Black a decisive attack despite the minus rook; for example 30 a4 Bf1! (threatening simply 31...h2!) 31 Rxf1 (or 31 Bh2 Qg4+ 32 Ke3 Re2+ etc) 31...Qg4+ 32 Ke3 Qe2+ mates, or 30 Bxc7 Qg4+ 31 Ke3 Qg5+ 32 Kf3 Be2+! 33 Rxe2 Qg4+ 34 Ke3 Rxe2+ 35 Kd3 Qf3+ 36 Kc4 Rxe4 and wins.

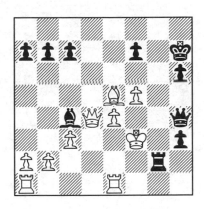

Diagram 19 (W)

Black has a decisive attack

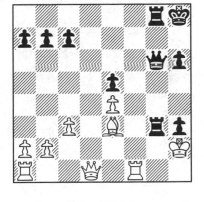

Diagram 20 (W)

There is no defence

25 Qd1

There doesn't seem to be a good defence for White:

a) 25 fxe6 Rxg3! 26 Kxg3 (or 26 Rf1 Qg6 27 exf7 Rg2+ 28 Kh1 Rh2+! etc) 26...Rg8+ 27 Kh2 Rg2+ 28 Kh1 Qf3 leads to mate.

b) 25 Rg1 Bxf5 26 Raf1 Rag8, threatening ...Qg7, is winning because 27 Rxf5 allows 27...Qxf5 28 exf5 Rxa4.

c) 25 Qc2 may be the best try, but then 25...Rag8 26 Rg1 Bd7 intending 27...Bc6 is very unpleasant.

25...Rag8 26 fxe6

After 26 Rg1 Black can simply play 26...Rxe4 27 fxe6 Rxe3.

26...Rxg3 27 exf7

Or 27 Qh5 Rxe3! 28 Qxf7 (if 28 Rxe3 Qf2+ 29 Kxh3 Qxe3+ mates) 28...Qg5 29 Qf2 Rg3 30 Rg1 Rg2+ 31 Rxg2 hxg2 32 Kg1 Qe7 and Black wins a couple of pawns.

27...Qxf7 28 Rf1 Qg6 0-1 (Diagram 20)

Black is threatening 29...Rg2+ 30 Kh1 Rh2+! etc, while after 29 Rg1 he has 29...Rg2+ 30 Kh1 Qg3 and mates.

Game 37
☐ V.Korchnoi ■ Z.Azmaiparashvili
Madrid 1996

---

1 Nf3 g6 2 e4 Bg7 3 d4 d6 4 c3 Nf6 5 Bd3 0-0 6 0-0 Nc6 7 b4 (Diagram 21)

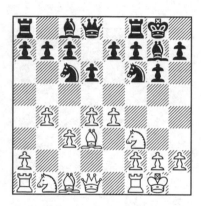
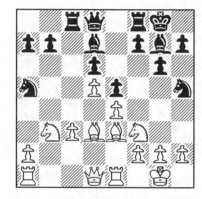

Diagram 21 (B)	**Diagram 22 (W)**
Weakening the long diagonal	Gaining counterplay on the c-file

 NOTE: Although this move gains space it weakens White's position along the key h8-a1 diagonal. Watch out for combinative possibilities there if White plays this move against you.

7...Nh5

This apparently far-flung knight sortie helps prepare ...e7-e5 whilst bringing the knight in contact with the f4-square.

8 b5

If 8 Be3 e5 9 d5 Ne7 10 c4 f5 with a good game for Black.

8...Na5 9 Re1 c5 10 bxc6 Nxc6 11 Be3 e5 12 d5

There's a case for trying to maintain the pawn centre with 12 Nbd2, but then 12...d5!? 13 dxe5 (13 exd5 exd4! 14 cxd4 Qxd5 15 Bc4 Qd8 is also fine for Black) 13...Nxe5 14 Nxe5 Bxe5 would be unclear.

12...Na5 13 Nbd2 Bd7 14 Nb3 Rc8! (Diagram 22) 15 Nxa5

Perhaps White should have chosen 15 Bxa7, though after 15...Rxc3 16 Qd2 Rxb3 17 axb3 Nxb3 18 Qb4 Nxa1 19 Rxa1 Nf4 20 Bf1 f5!? 21 Qxd6 fxe4 22 Ng5 Bf5 Black once again has active play.

15...Qxa5 16 c4 f5!

As always this is a key pawn lever once White has closed the centre with d4-d5.

17 Bd2

Now Black gets a very comfortable game with simple and logical moves. So perhaps White should have offered the exchange at this point with 17 exf5!?, for example 17...e4 18 Bxe4 Bxa1 19 Qxa1 Bxf5 20 Nd2 Bxe4 21 Nxe4 Rxc4 22 Nxd6 with messy play.

17...Qc7 18 Rc1 fxe4 19 Bxe4 Nf6 20 Bb1 Bg4 21 h3 Bxf3 22 Qxf3 Nd7 23 Qg3 Nc5 (Diagram 23)

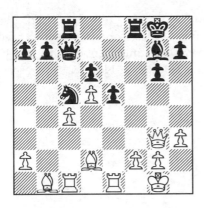

Diagram 23 (W)

The knight is a tower of strength

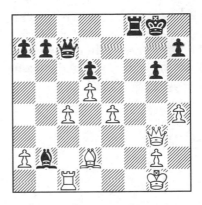

Diagram 24 (W)

Difficult to defend

24 h4 Rce8 25 f3?!

In view of Black's powerful reply, maybe White should have played 25 Be4 here.

25...e4! 26 Bxe4 Nxe4

Trying to win the exchange with 26...Bd4+?! 27 Kh1 Bf2? 28 Qxf2 Nxe4 29 Qd4 Ng3+ 30 Kh2 Ne2 would backfire badly after 31 Rxe2 Rxe2 32 Bc3.

27 Rxe4

27 fxe4 Bd4+ 28 Be3 Rxe4 29 Bxd4 Rxd4 30 c5 might have been a better line, but not 30 Re6 Qc5 31 Rxg6+?? Kh8! and wins.

27...Rxe4 28 fxe4 Bb2! (Diagram 24) 29 Rb1?

White should have played 29 Rc2, for example 29...Bd4+ 30 Be3 Qb6 31 Bxd4 Qxd4+ 32 Rf2 (32 Kh2? Qxe4 33 Rc1 Rf4 is more unpleasant) 32...b6 33 h5 Qd1+ 34 Kh2 Rxf2 35 Qxf2 Qxh5+ 36 Kg1 with a slightly worse but defensible queen endgame. However, Korchnoi was characteristically short of time by this point.

29...Qxc4 30 Bh6??

Losing immediately; while if 30 Rxb2?? Qd4+ picks up the rook. 30 Re1 was probably best, but after 30...Qxa2 Black has two connected passed pawns on the queenside.

30...Bd4+ 31 Be3 Qc3! 32 Re1 Be5 0-1

Summary

By playing c2-c3 White is showing the Modern considerably more respect (or fear?) by attempting to blunt Black's bishop on g7. On the other hand this quiet move does not have that much aggressive potential.

Black gets a decent game by playing ...Nc6 and heading for ...e7-e5, perhaps playing a preliminary ...Nfd7 or ...Nh5 so as to be able to recapture on e5 with a piece. In the lines where White plays Bg5 this bishop can be hunted down with ...h7-h6, ...g6-g5 and ...Nh5; whilst the strongest medicine (Hodgson-Norwood) is reserved for the aggressive f2-f4.

Chapter Eight

The Averbakh System

▨ **Introduction**

▨ **Illustrative Games**

Introduction

The former World Champion Mikhail Botvinnik felt that putting pawns on c4, d4 and e4, sometimes known as the Averbakh System, was White's strongest set-up against the Modern Defence. White takes a lion's share of space in the centre and Black must create counterplay in order to avoid strangulation. I used to play the move 4...Nc6, immediately counterattacking d4, but later switched to a far more sneaky approach.

1 d4 g6 2 c4 Bg7 3 e4

Another possibility is 3 Nc3 d6 4 Bg5, which I met with 4...h6 5 Bh4 c5 6 d5 Bxc3+ 7 bxc3 Nf6 in Taeger-Davies, Calella 1981 (see Game 38).

3...d6 4 Nc3 a6!? (Diagram 1)

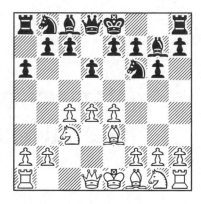

Diagram 1 (W)	Diagram 2 (W)
An ubiquitous little move	Going into a King's Indian

Once again we see this ubiquitous little move. The main idea is to expand on the queenside with ...c7-c6 and ...b7-b5, but if White puts his knight on f3 a different plan comes into operation.

5 Be3

Aiming for a Sämisch type set-up, though many other moves are possible:

a) 5 f4 is the most direct attempt to refute Black's play, but this backfired badly in Thomas-Davies, British Championship 1984 (Game 39).

b) 5 d5 c6 (5...Bxc3+ 6 bxc3 Nf6 7 Bd3 Nbd7 looks pretty good to me now) 6 Bd3 Nf6 7 Nge2 Nbd7 8 0-0 Ne5 9 Kh1 0-0 10 f3 Nfd7 11 f4 Nxd3 12 Qxd3 Nc5 and Black had at least equalized in A.Gokhale-N.Davies, Scarborough 1999.

c) 5 Nf3 Bg4 is one of the main points behind 4...a6. Then 6 Be2 Nc6 7 d5 (7 Be3 can be met by 7...e5 8 d5 Bxf3 9 Bxf3 Nd4, for example 10 0-0 Ne7 11 Bxd4 exd4 12 Ne2 c5) 7...Bxf3 8 Bxf3 Nd4 9 Be3 Nxf3+ 10 Qxf3 Nf6 11 0-0 0-0 12 Rad1 Nd7 was about equal in Tozer-Davies, ARC Young Masters 1987 (Game 40).

d) 5 h3 is a clever move, recognizing Black's idea of ...Bg4 while keeping f3 available for the knight on g1. In reply 5...c6!? is very interesting, just playing to expand on the queenside with ...b7-b5, for example 6 Nf3 b5 7 a3 Nd7 8 Be3 Rb8 9 c5 dxc5 10 dxc5 Qc7 11 Qd2 Ngf6 was OK for Black in R.Vera-A.Zlochevskij, Porto San Giorgio 1998.

Previously in my own games I've chosen to go into a King's Indian with 5...Nf6 **(Diagram 2)**; for example 6 Nf3 (6 Bg5 0-0 7 a4 a5 is Game 41, Neffe-Davies) 6...0-0 7 Be3 c6 8 Bd3 b5 9 0-0 bxc4 (9...Nbd7 10 e5 Ne8 11 exd6 exd6 12 Rc1 Nc7 13 Bg5 ½-½ was R.Pert-N.Davies, Birmingham 2005, but White is better in the final position) 10 Bxc4 d5 11 Bd3 dxe4 12 Nxe4 Nd5 13 Bg5 Qb6 (13...Bf5 looks OK here too) 14 Nc3 Qxb2 15 Nxd5 cxd5 16 Bxe7 Re8 17 Re1 was V.Zvjaginsev-N.Davies, Calcutta 1997, and now 17...Bxd4 (rather than 17...Nc6) 18 Nxd4 Qxd4 19 Bb4 Bd7 20 Qd2 Nc6 is about equal.

5...Nf6

To be honest I don't like this move as much as the immediate ...c7-c6, since developing the knight on f6 so soon seems to invite an early e4-e5 by White in many lines. After 5...c6 the game would in all probability transpose below after 6 Bd3 (6 c5 b5 7 cxb6 Qxb6 8 Qd2 Nf6 9 f3 0-0 10 Bc4 a5 11 Nge2 Ba6 12 Bxa6 Qxa6 was fine for Black in J.Levitt-N.Davies, Southend 1999) 6...b5 7 Nge2 Nf6 8 f3 etc; though in D.Mote-N.Davies, Chicago 1996, White played the dubious 8 d5?!, when 8...bxc4 9 Bxc4 0-0 10 0-0 Ng4 11 Bf4 Ne5 12 Bb3 Nbd7 13 dxc6 Nxc6 was very comfortable for Black.

6 f3 c6 7 Bd3 b5 (Diagram 3)

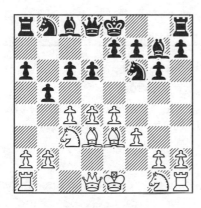
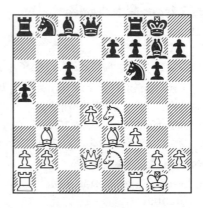

Diagram 3 (W)
The Byrne System

Diagram 4 (B)
White is slightly better

The characteristic move of the Byrne System against the Sämisch.

8 Qd2

Instead:

a) 8 e5 Nfd7 9 f4 bxc4 10 Bxc4 Nb6 11 Bd3 a5 12 Nf3 Na6 13 a3 Nc7 14 0-0 Ncd5 was about equal in G.Nikolaou-E.Grivas, Athens 2000.

b) 8 Nge2 is another possibility, when 8...0-0 9 0-0 Nbd7 10 b3 (10 Qd2 transposes to the next note) 10...bxc4 11 Bxc4 a5 12 Rc1 Nb6 13 Bd3 Ba6 14 Nb1 Bb7 15 Nbc3 Nfd7 16 Kh1 e6 gave Black a comfortable position in Bu Xiangzhi-B.Jobava, Moscow 2002.

8...bxc4?!

An instructive error. I think that Black should delay this with just 8...0-0 9 Nge2 Nbd7 10 0-0 e5 11 a4 bxc4 (11...exd4 12 Nxd4 b4 13 Na2 Qc7 is playable here too) 12 Bxc4 Rb8 13 Rfd1 Re8 14 a5 Qc7 15 Na4?! d5! 16 exd5 cxd5 17 Ba2 Bb7 and Black stood well in Tagesson-Davies, Osterskars 1995 (Game 43).

9 Bxc4 d5 10 Bb3 dxe4 11 Nxe4?!

White has a stronger move in 11 fxe4!, for example 11...Ng4 (or if 11...e5 12 Nf3! with a clear advantage – Botvinnik) 12 Nf3 Nxe3 13 Qxe3 0-0 14 h4 Bg4 15 h5 Bxh5 16 0-0-0 and White had a very dangerous attacking position in Z.Vranesic-P.Benko, Ottawa 1964.

11...0-0 12 Ne2 a5 13 0-0 (Diagram 4)

and White was slightly better in Botvinnik-Smyslov, Moscow 1958 (see Game 42).

Illustrative Games

Game 38
□ **W.Taeger** ■ **N.Davies**
Calella 1981

1 d4 g6 2 c4 Bg7 3 Nc3 d6 4 Bg5 h6 5 Bh4 c5 6 d5 Bxc3+ (Diagram 5)

Giving up the bishop but damaging White's pawn structure.

Another interesting possibility is 6...Qa5 7 Qd2 f5, for example 8 e3 Nd7 9 f4 Bxc3 10 bxc3 Ngf6 11 Bd3 Nb6 12 Bxf6 exf6 13 a4 Bd7 14 Ne2 Nxa4 15 g4 was very messy in I.Sokolov-V.Jansa, Copenhagen 1991.

7 bxc3 Nf6 8 f3 Qa5 9 Qd2

9 Qb3 would lend better protection to the weak pawn on c4 but with less aggressive potential.

9...Nbd7 10 e4 b6 11 Nh3 Ba6

Making a beeline for the pawn on c4. Black's threats include 12...Ne5 and 12...Qa4.

12 Be2 Qa4 13 0-0 Bxc4 14 Bxc4 Qxc4 15 a4 g5 16 Bg3 a5

These days I wouldn't play such a move. 16...g4 is a much better idea.

17 Rfe1 0-0-0 18 Nf2 h5!? (Diagram 6) 19 Qxg5 h4 20 Bxh4 Rdg8 21 Qf4 Nxd5 22 Qd2?!

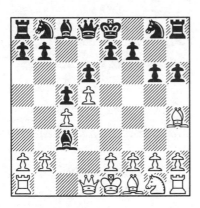

Diagram 5 (W)

Wrecking White's pawn structure

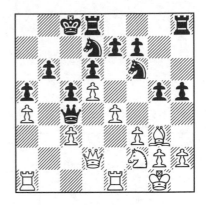

Diagram 6 (W)

Returning material for the initiative

My idea was that, after 22 Qxf7, Black has 22...Rxg2+ and 23 Kxg2? Ne3+ wins the queen; but White can also play 23 Kh1, when 23...Rgg8 24 Qxd5 Qxd5 (24...Qxc3 is answered by 25 Nd3) 25 exd5 Rxh4 26 Ng4 is probably about equal.

22...Rxh4 23 exd5?

With his king vulnerable White should get the queens off: after 23 Qxd5 Qxd5 24 exd5 Ne5 25 Kh1 it's still not bad for White.

23...Ne5 24 Qe3 Qxd5 25 Kh1 Qc6 (Diagram 7)

A pawn up and with the better position, the only problem for Black is his own weakened king.

26 Qe2 Kb7 27 Nd3 Ng6 28 h3 e6 29 Qf2 Rxa4

That makes it two pawns.

30 Rxa4 Qxa4 31 Rb1 Kc7 32 Qd2 Rb8 33 Nf2 Qf4 34 Qe2 c4 35 Ng4 d5 36 Ne3 Qd6 37 Rd1 Nf4 38 Qa2 Qc6 39 Rd4 e5 40 Nxd5+ Kb7 41 Ne7 Qe6 42 Rxc4 Qxe7 (Diagram 8)

With an extra piece it's starting not to matter about Black's slightly exposed king. White could have saved himself the rest.

43 Qb1 Qd7 44 Rc5 Qd3 45 Qxd3 Nxd3 46 Rd5 Nc1 47 Rxe5 Ra8

Rook behind the passed pawn.

48 Re7+ Kc6 49 Rxf7 a4 50 Re7 a3 51 Re1 0-1

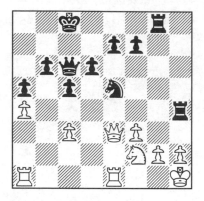

Diagram 7 (W)	**Diagram 8 (W)**
Black is a pawn up	White could resign here

Game 39
☐ **N.Thomas** ■ **N.Davies**
British Championship, Brighton 1984

---

1 e4 g6 2 d4 Bg7 3 c4 d6 4 Nc3 a6 5 f4

> **WARNING: When White throws pawns forward like this the position can become critical early on. If you can break up White's pawn centre the gaping holes in his ranks can tell against him. On the other hand, you can get suffocated if White consolidates his space advantage.**

5...c6 6 a4 (Diagram 9)

This is one way to stop ...b7-b5, but it gives Black the b4-square.

A natural alternative is 6 Nf3, after which 6...b5 7 a3 Bb7 8 e5 (8 Be2 Nd7 9 0-0 Nb6!? 10 b3 Nh6 has a certain dadaistic appeal; nobody is denying the fact that White has 'space', but pawns as always cannot move backwards) 8...Nh6 9 Be2 0-0 10 0-0 Qb6 (or 10...Nd7) 11 Kh1 Nf5 12 g4 Nh6 led to a very complex game in L.Popov-M.Ujtelky, Budapest 1960.

6...a5 7 Nf3 Bg4 8 Be2 Qb6 9 e5 Nh6

Targeting the newly weakened f5-square, from where the knight can put pressure on the d4-pawn.

10 Ng5

Another possibility is 10 Nh4 Bxe2 11 Qxe2 Nd7 (if 11...Qxd4?? 12 Be3 traps the queen) 12 Be3 (12 exd6?! 0-0 13 dxe7 Rfe8 leaves White's position horribly exposed), when Black can try 12...Qb4 intending ...Nb6-c4.

10...Bxe2 11 Qxe2 Nf5 12 exd6? (Diagram 10)

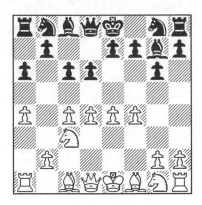

Diagram 9 (B)

Ceding the b4-square

Diagram 10 (B)

Trying to force matters

White should have tried to 'defend' his space with 12 Nf3, but then 12...dxe5 (12...h5 is also possible) 13 dxe5 Na6 14 g4 Nh6 would once again leave White's position full of holes.

12...0-0 13 dxe7

Or if 13 c5 Qb4 14 Bd2 exd6 15 cxd6 Qxd6 and Black is clearly better.

13...Re8 14 0-0 Rxe7 15 Qd3 Na6 16 Kh1 Qxd4 17 Qxd4 Nxd4 (Diagram 11)

18 Bd2

After 18 Nf3 Nxf3 19 gxf3 f5! White's position would be strategically bankrupt.

18...Nb3 19 Rad1 Rd8 20 Be1

If 20 Rfe1 Rxe1+ 21 Bxe1 Rxd1 22 Nxd1 Nac5 and Black would start rounding up the queenside pawns.

20...Rxd1 21 Nxd1 f5

Preventing f4-f5.

22 h3 Nac5 23 Nc3 Nd3 24 Bh4 Re8

24...Nxb2 is also good, but there's no hurry.

25 Nd1 Nd2 26 Rg1 Nxc4 27 Nf3 0-1 (Diagram 12)

White has understandably had enough.

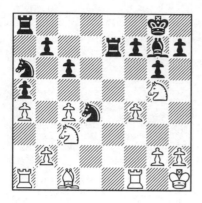

Diagram 11 (W)

White's position is full of holes

Diagram 12 (B)

White has had enough

Game 40
□ **R.Tozer** ■ **N.Davies**
ARC Young Masters, Westergate 1987

---

1 d4 d6 2 c4 g6 3 Nc3 Bg7 4 e4 a6 5 Nf3 (Diagram 13)

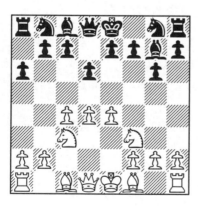

Diagram 13 (B)

Black can pin the knight

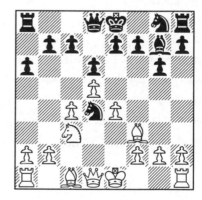

Diagram 14 (W)

The point of Black's play

This looks like the most 'natural' and 'sensible' move, but it is also one which falls in with Black's last move.

5...Bg4

Black can still play 5...c6 6 Be2 b5, though after 7 a3 Bb7 8 0-0 Nd7 9 Be3 e6 10 d5 he was skating on thin ice in J.Penrose-N.Botvinnik, Hastings 1966/67.

6 Be2 Nc6 7 d5

One of the points of this 4...a6 line is that after 7 Be3 e5 8 d5 Bxf3 9 Bxf3 Nd4 10 Bxd4 exd4 White cannot play his knight to b5. My analysis continues 11 Ne2 c5 (11...Qf6 12 Qb3 0-0-0 13 0-0-0 may be less good as Black's d4-pawn is weak) 12 dxc6 bxc6 13 Nxd4 Qa5+ 14 Kf1 Qc5 15 e5 Ne7 16 Qa4 0-0 17 Nxc6 Nxc6 18 Qxc6 Qxe5 19 Rb1 Qa5 with adequate compensation for the pawn due to Black's active pieces and White's loss of castling rights.

One other possibility is 7 Ng1, when Black can play 7...Bd7 8 Be3 e5 9 Nf3 exd4 (or 9...Bg4!?) 10 Nxd4 Nge7 with adequate counterplay. This is like one of the lines arising from 4...e5, but with the extra move ...Bc8-d7 for Black.

7...Bxf3 8 Bxf3 Nd4 (Diagram 14) 9 Be3

9 0-0 c5 10 dxc6 bxc6 11 c5 dxc5 12 Be3 was D.Gurevich-B.Züger, Geneva 1999, and now Black should have made the defence of d4 and c5 his top priority with 12...Qb8 or maybe 12...Be5. Instead he played 12...Nf6, after which 13 Na4 Nd7 14 Bg4 e6 15 Rc1 h5 16 Be2 0-0 17 Nxc5 Nxc5 18 Rxc5 Qd6 19 Rc4 was slightly better for White.

9...Nxf3+

Another option is 9...c5 10 dxc6 Nxc6, but this looks a bit better for White after 11 Rc1 Nf6 12 0-0 0-0 13 Be2 Nd7 14 Qd2 Nc5 15 f3 Ne6 16 Rfd1 as in a game L.Kritz-F.Jenni, Zug 2001.

10 Qxf3 Nf6 11 0-0 0-0 12 Rad1 Nd7 13 Qh3

Preventing 13...e5 and playing for the attack. This is one of the effects of playing small moves with one's a-pawn: very often White will try very hard to punish you.

13...Ne5 14 Bh6

White can't defend c4 with 14 b3 because 14...Nxc4 wins a pawn anyway. However, 14 c5 was interesting, for example 14...Nc4 15 Bh6 Bxh6 16 Qxh6 dxc5 17 Rd3 f6 18 Rh3 Rf7. White has compensation for his pawn, but it's not clear that it's enough.

14...Nxc4 15 Bxg7 Kxg7 16 b3 Nb6 17 f4 Nd7 (Diagram 15)

Returning to the kingside to help defend his monarch.

18 Rd3 e5 19 f5 f6

There were other possibilities here in 19...Nf6 and 19...g5. In any case Black is OK.

20 fxg6 hxg6 21 Rg3 Rh8 22 Qg4 Nf8 23 Nd1 Qd7 24 Qf3 Nh7 25 Ne3 Rag8 26 Nf5+ Kf8 27 Nh4

After 27 Nh6 Rg7 Black would continue the evacuation of his king to the queen-side.

27...Qf7 28 Qg4 Ng5 29 Rc3 Kg7 30 Rfc1 Rc8 31 Nf3 Nxf3+ 32 Rxf3 Rce8 33 Rcf1 Ref8 (Diagram 16) 34 Rxf6

Diagram 15 (W)

Returning to the defence

Diagram 16 (W)

White cannot make progress

White's back and forth threats are not making much of an impression, so he tries his luck in the queen vs two rooks position.

34...Qxf6 35 Rxf6 Rxf6 36 g3 Rhf8 37 Kg2?

37 Qe2 was the right move, though Black is still in the driving seat.

37...Rf2+ 38 Kg1 Rxa2 39 Qd7+ Rf7 40 Qc8 b5 41 h4 a5 42 Qg4?

After this White's king is caught in a net. 42 Qb7 would have been more tenacious.

42...Raf2 43 Qg5?! Rf1+ 44 Kg2 R7f2+ 45 Kh3 Rh1+ 46 Kg4 Rf4+! 47 gxf4 Rg1+ 0-1

The coming pawn endgame is hopeless for White.

Game 41
□ A.Neffe ■ N.Davies
Wrexham 1995

---

1 e4 g6 2 d4 Bg7 3 c4 d6 4 Nc3 a6 5 h3 Nf6

In retrospect I prefer 5...c6 in this position.

6 Bg5

As I mentioned in the introduction I've had 6 Nf3 played against me in a couple of games, the one with Zvjaginsev being something I'd prefer to forget. But Black's problems come from the possibility of e4-e5, which is why it's better to delay ...Ng8-f6.

6...0-0 7 a4?! (Diagram 17)

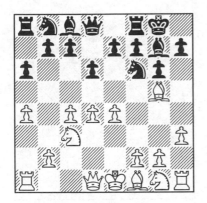

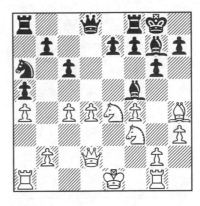

Diagram 17 (B)	**Diagram 18 (W)**
Weakening the queenside	Black is clearly better

This is a gratuitous weakening of White's queenside. It is especially poor given the fact that Black wasn't even 'threatening' ...b7-b5.

7...a5

 TIP: When White has played c2-c4 and a2-a4, it's often good to control the b4-square with ...a7-a5 and then later plant a knight on it.

8 f4

I'm always happy to see moves like this. Pawns don't go backwards.

8...c6 9 Nf3 Nh5!

Threatening the f4-pawn with 10...f6, while also preparing to hop into g3. White's position is already looking seriously exposed.

10 Qd2 d5!?

Trying to open it up, even at the cost of a material investment.

11 Bd3

After 11 exd5 Black would have had several attractive possibilities, e.g. 11...Ng3 12 Rg1 cxd5 13 Nxd5 Nc6 14 Bd3 Be6 15 Kf2 Nf5 16 Bxf5 gxf5 and Black will recover the pawn with a good game. Even so this was probably better than the text.

11...Ng3 12 Rg1 dxe4 13 Bxe4 Na6 14 Bh4 Nxe4 15 Nxe4 Bf5 (Diagram 18)

With a nice bishop pair and White unable to castle short, Black's position is much to be preferred.

16 Ng3 Be6 17 Rc1 Qb6 18 f5?!

Trying to shoot his way out of trouble, but this is a pawn.

18...Bxf5 19 Nxf5 gxf5 20 g4 f4 21 Qxf4 Qxb2 22 Kf1 Nb4 23 Qe3 e5! (Diagram 19)

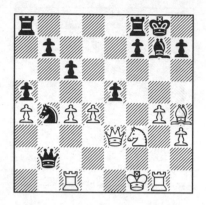

Diagram 19 (W)

Time to stick the boot in

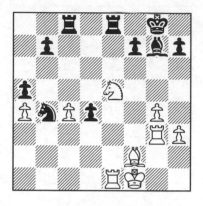

Diagram 20 (W)

Black is winning

With White's king so exposed it's time to stick the boot in.

24 Nxe5?

After 24 dxe5 a sample line is 24...Nd3 25 Rd1 Nxe5 26 Nxe5 Rae8 27 Nd3 Rxe3 28 Nxb2 Rxh3 29 Bg3 Bxb2 going two pawns up.

24...c5

Undermining the knight on e5. Another good line was 24...f6 25 Nf3 Rae8.

25 Re1 cxd4 26 Qf2 Qxf2+ 27 Bxf2 Rac8 28 Rg3 Rfe8 (Diagram 20) 29 Nd3

29 Bxd4? gets stomped on by 29...Nc2.

29...Rxe1+ 30 Bxe1 Nc2 31 Bxa5 Ne3+ 32 Rxe3?!

A bit of desperation that makes Black's job easier.

32...dxe3 33 c5 Ra8 34 Bb6 Rxa4 35 Ke2 Bd4 36 Nf4 Bxc5 37 Bxc5 Rxf4 38 Bxe3 Re4 0-1

Game 42

☐ **M.Botvinnik** ■ **V.Smyslov**

World Championship (6th matchgame), Moscow 1958

---

1 c4 g6 2 e4 Bg7 3 d4 d6 4 Nc3 a6 5 Be3 Nf6

As I mentioned in the introduction I think that 5...c6 is a better move.

6 f3 c6 (Diagram 21)

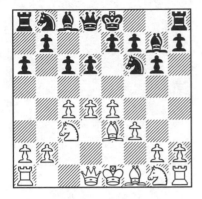

Diagram 21 (W)

Intending ...b7-b5

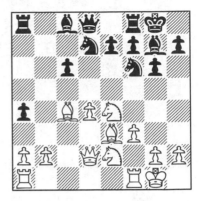

Diagram 22 (W)

Black has a good position

7 Bd3

Smyslov's move order with 5...Nf6 (rather than 5...c6) makes 7 e5!? promising.

7...b5 8 Qd2 bxc4?!

 WARNING: Black should not be in too much of a hurry to play this move as it helps White activate his pieces. I prefer to keep the tension with 8...0-0 or 8...Nbd7 (see the next game).

9 Bxc4 d5 10 Bb3 dxe4 11 Nxe4?!

11 fxe4 is stronger here, as noted in the introduction. Botvinnik's move gives Black the valuable d5 outpost.

11...0-0 12 Ne2 a5 13 0-0 a4 14 Bc4 Nbd7 (Diagram 22)

Black has established quite a good position with an outpost on d5 and the chance of play along the b-file.

Another, possibly superior option was 14...Nxe4 15 fxe4 c5 16 Bh6 Bg4 17 Bxg7 Kxg7 18 Qc3 (if 18 Rxf7+ Rxf7 19 Bxf7 Bxe2 20 Bd5 Ra6 21 Qxe2 e6) 18...cxd4 19 Nxd4 e5 as in A.O'Kelly-P.Dubinin, correspondence 1959.

15 Rac1 Rb8 16 Nxf6+ Bxf6 17 Nc3 Nb6 18 Be2 Be6 19 Rfd1 Bg7

According to Botvinnik Black should have played 19...Qd7 20 Bf1 Rfd8 with a slight edge. As the game goes he gradually outplays his great rival.

20 Bh6 Bxh6 21 Qxh6 f6 22 Rd2 Bf7 23 h4 Qd7 24 a3 Rfd8 25 Ne4 Qe8 26 Bf1 Bd5 27 Nc5 Qf8 28 Qxf8+ Kxf8 29 Na6! (Diagram 23)

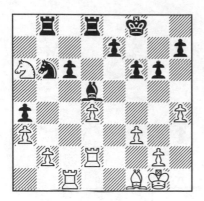

Diagram 23 (B)

The knight heads for b4

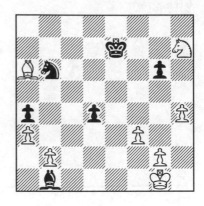

Diagram 24 (B)

Precision to the end

This knight is coming to the wonderful b4-square, from where it will put pressure on c6.

29...Rbc8 30 Nb4 Bb3 31 Rxc6 Rxc6 32 Nxc6 Rd6 33 Na5 Ba2

After 33...e5 34 Nxb3 axb3 35 Rd3! White would get two connected passed pawns and win easily.

34 Nb7 Rd5 35 Nc5 e5 36 Ne4 Rxd4 37 Rxd4 exd4 38 Nxf6 Ke7

38...Bc4? is much worse due to 39 Nd7+, establishing an easily won bishop vs knight ending.

39 Nxh7 Bb1 40 Ba6! (Diagram 24)

40 Kf2? d3 41 Ng5 d2 42 Ke2 Bd3+! shows that accurate play is still required.

40...Nd5 41 Kf2 Ne3 42 Be2 Ke6 43 Ng5+ Kd5 44 Ne4 Bxe4 45 fxe4+ Kxe4 46 g4 Kf4 47 h5 gxh5 48 gxh5 Kg5 49 Kf3 1-0

Establishing a distant passed pawn which decides the game. While Black's king guards against its further advance, White's monarch will devour his two remaining pawns.

Game 43
☐ **B.Tagesson** ■ **N.Davies**
Osterskars 1995

---

1 e4 g6 2 d4 Bg7 3 c4 d6 4 Nc3 a6 5 Be3 c6 6 f3 b5 7 Qd2 Nd7 8 Bd3 Ngf6 (Diagram 25)

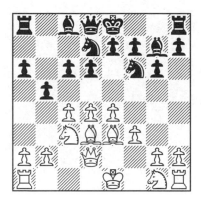
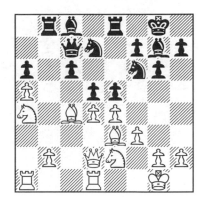

| **Diagram 25 (W)** | **Diagram 26 (W)** |
| A satisfactory King's Indian | Striking in the centre |

 NOTE: Reaching a satisfactory version of the Sämisch King's Indian.

9 Nge2 0-0 10 0-0 e5 11 a4

Another possibility is 11 b3, when H.Ree-R.Byrne, Wijk aan Zee 1980, continued 11...exd4 12 Nxd4 Ne5 13 Be2 c5 14 Nc2 bxc4 15 bxc4 Be6 16 Nd5 Nxd5 17 exd5 Bd7 with approximate equality.

11...bxc4

I preferred this to 11...b4 because I wanted to keep the b-file open, but the advance of Black's b-pawn is also eminently playable. S.Smetankin-V.Sergeev, Polanica Zdroj 2001, went 12 Nd1 exd4 13 Nxd4 Qc7 14 Nf2 Ne5 15 Be2 c5 16 Nb3 Be6 17 Qc2 Rfe8 18 Rad1 a5 again with rough equality.

12 Bxc4 Rb8 13 Rfd1 Re8 14 a5 Qc7 15 Na4

After this decentralizing move Black gets to strike in the centre. 15 b3 would have been a steadier choice.

15...d5! (Diagram 26) 16 exd5 cxd5 17 Ba2 Bb7 18 Rac1 Qd6 19 Nc5?!

White should have admitted his 15th move was mistaken and played 19 Nac3. But it's never easy to retract like this.

19...Nxc5 20 dxc5

Now Black gets a mobile central pawn majority whilst White's queenside pawns will find it difficult to advance. Perhaps White got worried that after 20 Rxc5 Black can play 20...Ng4!?, when the sequel 21 fxg4 exd4 22 Bxd4 Rxe2 23 Qxe2 Bxd4+ 24 Rxd4 Qxc5 regains the material with the advantage due to White's weakened king. But this was preferable to the game.

20...Qd7 21 Nc3 d4 22 Bg5 Qc7 (Diagram 27)

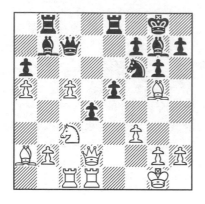

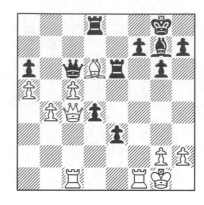

Diagram 27 (W)

The central pawns are stronger

Diagram 28 (B)

Losing quickly

22...Bc6 is better, stopping White's knight from coming to a4. In the game White avoids this, perhaps because his earlier Nc3-a4 had been unsuccessful.

23 Ne4?

Giving a pawn away for nothing. 23 Na4 was stronger, though I still prefer Black after 23...Bd5 24 Bxd5 Nxd5 25 Nb6 Qc6. As usual the problem for White is that his queenside pawns cannot easily advance.

23...Nxe4 24 fxe4 Bxe4 25 Rf1 Bf5 26 Bc4

26 c6 e4 would get ugly very quickly.

26...Qc6 27 Qe2

27 Bxf7+ Kxf7 28 g4 is tempting, but Black can just play 28...Kg8 29 gxf5 gxf5, the point being that after 30 Rxf5 h6 31 Bh4 Qg6+ he wins White's rook.

27...e4 28 b4 Be6 29 Bxe6 Rxe6 30 Qc4 e3 31 Bf4 Rd8 32 Bd6?! (Diagram 28)

This loses quickly, though by now it's difficult to give White good advice.

32...e2 33 Rfe1 Rexd6 34 cxd6 Qxc4 35 Rxc4 d3 0-1

Black will follow with 36...d2, winning a whole rook.

Summary

Space usually comes at the cost of certain weaknesses, and in playing the Averbakh System, by putting his pawns on c4 and e4, White weakens d4. In my early days with the Modern I tried to exploit this with 4...Nc6, but then later switched to the more subtle 4...a6!?. This keeps the option of playing against d4 (for instance after 5 Nf3 Bg4), while introducing the possibility of a queenside pawn advance. It's not easy to find moves for White which will inhibit both these options.

Chapter Nine

The Lesser Averbakh

- Introduction
- Illustrative Games

Introduction

After 1 d4 g6 2 c4 Bg7 the most usual continuation is 3 Nc3 d6 4 e4 (or 3 e4 d6 4 Nc3), which we looked at in the previous chapter. Developing the knight on f3 is a quieter option, indicating that White is looking more to maintain the space he has already taken rather than swamp Black altogether. One quite important point is that he keeps the possibility of defending d4 – Black's traditional point of counterattack – with the move e2-e3.

1 d4 g6 2 c4 Bg7 3 Nf3

3 Nc3 d6 4 Nf3 would come to the same thing.

3...d6 (Diagram 1)

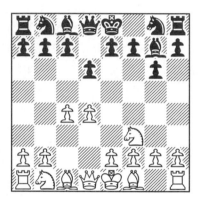

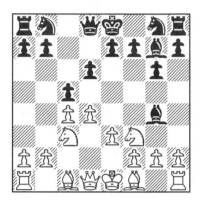

Diagram 1 (W)	Diagram 2 (W)
The Lesser Averbakh	Striking at the white centre

4 Nc3

White has two major alternatives: he can adopt a fianchetto with 4 g3, or take more space after all with 4 e4. But in both cases the delayed development of Black's king's knight gives him some definite pluses when compared with a King's Indian Defence:

a) 4 g3 can be effectively met with 4...e5, and the exchange of queens with 5 dxe5 dxe5 6 Qxd8+ Kxd8 gave White less than nothing in Pavlovic-Ivkov, Kladovo 1991 (Game 44). White could maintain the tension in the centre with 5 Nc3, say, but then 5...exd4 6 Nxd4 Ne7!, followed by 7...Nbc6, looks as if it would give Black very reasonable counterplay.

b) 4 e4 is logically answered by 4...Bg4!, intensifying the pressure on d4. After 5 Be2 Nc6 Black again got excellent counterplay in Vadasz-Adorjan, Hungary 1978 (see Game 45).

4...Bg4 5 e3

Reinforcing the d4-square hopes to prove that Black's early bishop manoeuvres are misconceived. Otherwise White can again play 5 g3, after which I like 5...Bxf3 6 exf3 e6! 7 Bg2 Ne7 as in Kaidanov-Vladimirov, Irkutsk 1983 (Game 46). Black is trying to mark the d4-pawn down as a weakness.

5...c5!? (Diagram 2)

This is the way I always play it with Black. In my opinion 5...c5 is the most logical move; the positioning of Black's bishops suggests that putting pressure on d4 has to be the plan.

6 Be2

Many Whites think they will have a good endgame after 6 dxc5 dxc5 7 Qxd8+, without seeing Black's important zwischenzug 6...Bxc3+ 7 bxc3 and only then 7...dxc5. In my opinion Black has the more promising chances in this position, as White's bishops are not working and his pawns may become lethally weak. In Mikhalevsky-Davies, Rishon LeZion 1995, I achieved a winning position after 8 Qxd8+ Kxd8 9 Ne5 Be6 10 e4 Nf6 11 Rb1 Nxe4 12 Rxb7 Nd6 13 Rb1 Nd7 14 Bf4 Nb6 15 Be2 f6 16 Nd3 Rc8 17 Bxd6 exd6 18 Nf4 Bf7 19 0-0 Kc7 20 Rfd1 Rb8 21 Rb3 Nxc4, but actually managed to lose (see Game 47).

Another major possibility is 6 d5, angling for a kind of Benoni in which White hopes that the bishop on g4 will be misplaced. I don't think it is and would even say that White has lost time with 5 e3 when really he would like this pawn on e4. Gausel-Jansa, Gausdal 1991, continued 6...Nf6 7 Be2 0-0 8 0-0 Na6 9 h3 Bxf3 10 Bxf3 Nc7 11 Rb1 Rb8 12 Be2 a6 13 a4 e5 14 dxe6 fxe6 with a very comfortable position for Black (see Game 48).

6...cxd4

This has been played almost exclusively in practice. I don't like 6...Nh6 because of 7 dxc5 Bxc3+ 8 bxc3 dxc5 9 Qxd8+ Kxd8 10 e4, when Black's knight on h6 has to retreat to g8 again.

7 exd4

The ambitious way to play it. 7 Nxd4 takes on fewer positional responsibilities but does not guarantee White a safe and easy life: 7...Bxe2 8 Ndxe2 Nf6 9 0-0 0-0 10 b3 Nc6 led eventually to a Black win in Dobosz-Jansa, Würzburg 1989 (Game 49).

7...Nh6!? (Diagram 3)

Pursuing the plan of attacking d4 with great determination. The knight wants to jump to f5.

8 h3 Bxf3 9 Bxf3 Nc6 10 d5 Ne5 11 Be2 Nf5 12 Bd2 0-0 13 0-0 a6 14 Re1 Qb6! (Diagram 4)

and Black's active pieces offset White's space and bishop pair in Portisch-Timman, Wijk aan Zee 1975 (Game 50).

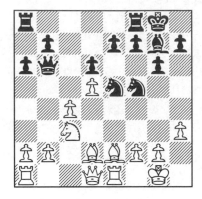

Diagram 3 (W)

Heading for f5 to attack d4

Diagram 4 (W)

Black has an active position

Illustrative Games

Game 44
□ **D.Pavlovic** ■ **B.Ivkov**
Yugoslav Championship, Kladovo 1991

1 d4 g6 2 Nf3 Bg7 3 c4 d6 4 g3 e5 5 dxe5 dxe5 6 Qxd8+ Kxd8 (Diagram 5)

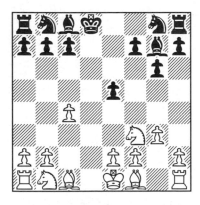

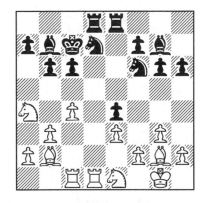

Diagram 5 (W)

White has no advantage

Diagram 6 (W)

Taking space in the centre

White has no advantage. In fact this kind of endgame can be dangerous for White because of the pawn on c4. In order to get a man-sized share of the centre White would like to play e2-e4, but this would now weaken the d4-square.

7 Bg2

J.Smejkal-R.Hübner, Amsterdam 1975, saw 7 Nc3 c6 8 Be3 Kc7 9 0-0-0 Na6 10 b4!? Nh6 (10...Nxb4?! 11 Bc5 Na6 12 Bd6+ Kb6 13 Kc2 would be very dangerous for Black) 11 b5 Nb8 12 Bc5 Rd8 13 Rxd8 (13 b6+ looks good but then 13...axb6 14 Bxb6+ Kxb6 15 Rxd8 Bd7 traps the rook on d8 and threatens 16...Kc7) 13...Kxd8 14 Bg2 Be6 15 Rd1+ Kc8 16 Ne4 Nd7 17 bxc6 bxc6 18 Ba3 Nf5 19 Nfg5 Bh6 20 e3 Bxc4 21 g4 Nh4 with approximate equality.

7...c6 8 0-0 Nd7

In K.Langeweg-B.Larsen, Beverwijk 1967, Black sacrificed a pawn with 8...Nh6 9 Bxh6 Bxh6 10 Nxe5 Be6, but had good compensation for it after 11 Nd2 Kc7 12 f4 Bg7 13 Nd3 Bd4+ 14 Kh1 Nd7 15 Rac1 Be3 16 Rfd1 h5.

9 Nc3 Ngf6 10 b3 h6 11 Bb2 Re8 12 e3 Kc7 13 Na4 b6 14 Rfd1 Bb7 15 Rac1 Rad8 16 Ne1 e4 (Diagram 6)

Taking space in the centre. Note that it was White's understandable reluctance to play e3-e4 which allowed this move by Black.

17 Bh3 Bc8 18 Bg2 Nh5 19 Bxg7 Nxg7 20 Nc3 f5 21 Rc2 Ne5 22 Rcd2 Rxd2 23 Rxd2 Ne6 (Diagram 7)

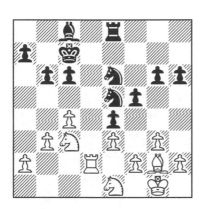
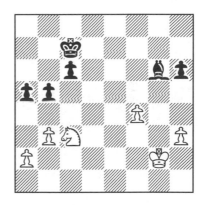

Diagram 7 (W)

Black is slightly better

Diagram 8 (W)

Black has a clear edge

Black is slightly better because of his extra space. It's instructive to see how the experienced Ivkov gradually nurtures this to victory.

24 Bf1 a5 25 Be2 Bd7 26 h3 Nc5 27 Kg2 Be6 28 f4

Making a bid for some freedom, but creating a weakness on e3 in the process.

28...exf3+ 29 Nxf3 Nxf3 30 Bxf3 g5 31 Rd4 Bf7 32 Kf2 Bg6 33 Rd1 f4 34 exf4 Nd3+ 35 Kg2 Ne1+ 36 Kf2 Nd3+ 37 Kg2 gxf4

The twofold repetition was a nice bit of Grandmasterly torture, dangling the draw in front of White and then snatching it away.

38 Be4?!

Immediately going wrong. White should have tried 38 Ne2 fxg3 39 Kxg3 Re3 40 Rf1, when there's still nothing clear for Black.

38...Rxe4! 39 Rxd3 Rxc4! 40 Rf3 Rd4 41 Rxf4 Rxf4 42 gxf4 b5 (Diagram 8)

The unbalanced pawns, plus bishop vs knight, give Black a clear edge.

43 a3?!

43 Kf3 is probably better, but White is still struggling after 43...Kd6.

43...b4 44 axb4 axb4 45 Na2 c5 46 Kf3 Kd6 47 Ke3 Kd5 48 Nc1 c4 49 Kd2 cxb3 50 Nxb3 Ke4

The b4-pawn keeps White tied down while his kingside gets eaten.

51 Na5 Kxf4 52 Nc6 b3 53 Kc3 Bc2 54 Ne7 Kg3 55 Ng8 h5 56 h4 Kxh4 57 Nf6 Kg5 0-1

Game 45
□ **L.Vadasz** ■ **A.Adorjan**
Hungary 1978

---

1 Nf3 g6 2 e4 Bg7 3 d4 d6 4 c4 Bg4! (Diagram 9)

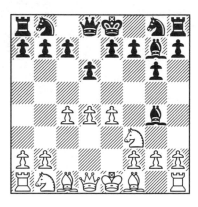

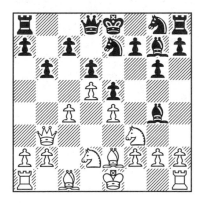

Diagram 9 (W)

Black makes a beeline for d4

Diagram 10 (W)

Initiating complex play

5 Be2 Nc6

In G.Kasparov-V.Anand, Moscow 1995, Black played an immediate 5...Bxf3, presumably to stop White either defending the knight with Nbd2 or playing Ng1 to exchange light-squared bishops. The game continued 6 Bxf3 Nc6 7 d5 Nd4 8 Nc3 c5 9 Be3 Qb6 10 Rb1 Nxf3+ 11 gxf3 Bxc3+ 12 bxc3 Qa6 13 Qe2 Nf6 14 e5 dxe5 15 Bxc5 Nd7 with an excellent position for Black.

6 Nbd2

This is an argument for Anand's 5...Bxf3, but Black seems to be OK in any case.

Two other moves are possible:

a) 6 Be3 e5 7 d5 Bxf3 8 Bxf3 Nd4 9 Bxd4 exd4 10 Na3 Ne7 11 0-0 c6 12 Rb1 0-0 13 Nc2 c5 14 b4 was L.Portisch-J.Timman, Candidates match, Antwerp 1989, and now rather than 14...Nc8 (as played in the game), 14...b6 would have been equal according to Timman.

b) 6 d5 Bxf3 7 Bxf3 Nd4 would transpose to the Kasparov-Anand game above.

6...e5 7 d5 Nce7

7...Bxf3 8 Nxf3 Nd4 is less good here because White has the two bishops. After 9 Nxd4 exd4 10 0-0 Ne7 11 Rb1, intending 12 b4 and 13 Bb2, White would have a clear advantage.

8 Qb3 b6!? (Diagram 10)

8...Qc8 or 8...Bc8 would be met by 9 c5!.

9 Nxe5! Bxe2 10 Qa4+ b5!

And not 10...Kf8? because of 11 Nd7+ Ke8 12 Nxb6+ and 13 Nxa8 etc.

11 Qxb5+ Kf8 12 Nd7+ Ke8 13 Nf6+

Not now 13 Nb6+? as 13...c6! wins a piece.

13...Kf8 14 Nxg8!?

Scorning the draw with 14 Nd7+ etc. Now if 14...Kxg8 15 Kxe2 or 14...Bd3 15 Nxe7 and White comes out at least one pawn up. Fortunately Black has a resource:

14...Nf5!! 15 exf5 Rb8! (Diagram 11) 16 Qxb8?

White had to play 16 Qa4, after which Adorjan gave the variation 16...Bd3 17 f6! Kxg8! 18 fxg7 Qe7+ 19 Ne4 Qxe4+ 20 Be3 Kxg7 21 0-0-0 Rxb2!? 22 Kxb2 Qe5+ 23 Ka3 Rb8 24 Qb3 (the only move) 24...Rxb3+ 25 axb3 Qc3! when the position is still far from clear, for example 26 Rhe1 c5! 27 Bd2 (27 dxc6 Qa5+ 28 Kb2 Qe5+ would be a draw by perpetual check) 27...Qc2 28 Ba5 Bxc4! 29 bxc4 Qxc4.

Now the game starts to crystallize in Black's favour.

16...Qxb8 17 Kxe2 Rxg8 18 Re1 Ke7!

Aiming to get the rook on g8 into play.

19 fxg6 hxg6 20 Kf1+ Kd7 21 Ne4 Re8 22 c5?!

Enterprisingly playing for the attack, but White should have been thinking about how to secure his position. 22 Rb1 would have offered greater chances to save the game, albeit fewer to win it.

22...Qb5+ 23 Kg1 dxc5

And not 23...f5? 24 c6+! when Black's king doesn't have a good square.

24 Bh6!? Bd4! 25 Rad1 Qxb2

25...f5? is still wrong because of 26 Rxd4! Rxe4 27 Rdxe4 fxe4 28 Bg7! and White will set up a fortress in the endgame.

26 Bc1

26 Rd2? runs into 26...Rxe4!.

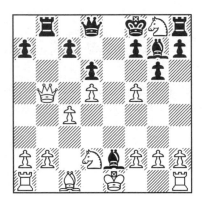

Diagram 11 (W)

What now for White?

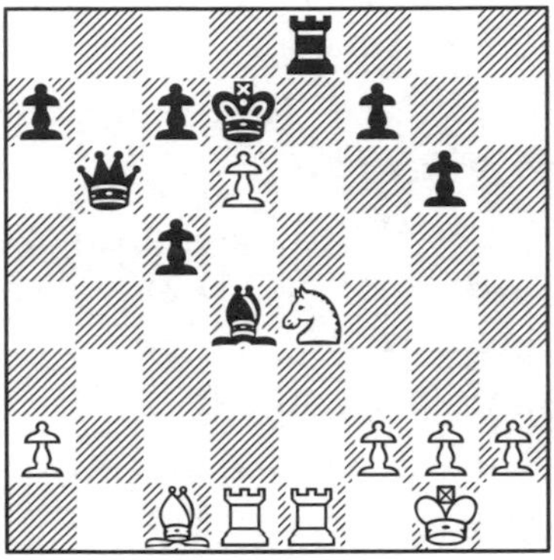

Diagram 12 (B)

Precision is still required

26...Qb6 27 d6! (Diagram 12) 27...Re6!

Precision is still required. White could save his skin after 27...cxd6? 28 Rxd4! cxd4 29 Nf6+ or 27...f5? 28 Nf6+!! Bxf6 29 dxc7+ Bd4 30 Rxe8.

28 dxc7 Kxc7 29 Bf4+ Kc6 30 h4 Qb2 31 Bg3 Qxa2

31...f5! was also good.

32 Kh2 a5 33 f3 a4 34 Rd2 Qb3 35 Rc1 Be3 36 Nxc5 Bxc5 0-1

In this losing position White's flag fell.

Game 46
□ **G.Kaidanov** ■ **E.Vladimirov**
Irkutsk 1983

---

1 d4 g6 2 c4 Bg7 3 Nc3 d6 4 Nf3 Bg4 5 g3 Bxf3 6 exf3 e6 (Diagram 13)

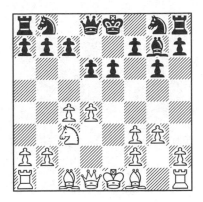

Diagram 13 (W)

The best set-up for Black

Diagram 14 (W)

The knights prepare to emerge

The best way to play the position, intending to develop the king's knight to e7. After that Black would be supporting ...d6-d5, while the knight can also come to f5 to help put pressure on d4.

7 Bg2 Ne7 8 0-0 0-0 9 Re1

E.Geller-A.Kochyev, Lvov 1978, varied with the immediate 9 d5, when 9...e5 10 f4 Nd7 11 Bh3 a5 12 Re1 Nf5! 13 fxe5 dxe5 14 Ne4 b6 15 Bg5 f6 16 Bd2 Nd6 17 Be6+ Kh8 18 Nxd6 cxd6 19 f4 f5 brought about a sharp position in which Black's dark-squared bishop was very strong.

9...Nd7 10 d5

Although this pawn becomes weak White doesn't want to wait for his opponent to blockade it with ...c7-c6 and ...d6-d5.

10...exd5 11 cxd5 Re8 (Diagram 14) 12 Bh3

12 g4 also stops Black's e7-knight coming to f5, but weakens the kingside. Meanwhile there's still another target for Black: the d5-pawn. L.Van Wely-V.Tkachiev, Neum 2000, continued 12...Nb6 13 f4 c6 14 dxc6 bxc6 15 Ne4 d5 16 Nc5 Qd6 17 Nb7 Qc7 18 Nc5 Qd6 19 Nb7 Qc7 20 Nc5 Nc4 (rejecting the draw by repetition) 21 Re2, and now 21...Qb6 (rather than 21...Rad8) was probably best.

12...Nb6

Honing in on the d5-pawn.

13 Qd3 Bxc3

Obviously this involves weakening the dark squares around Black's king, but a pawn is a pawn.

14 bxc3 Nexd5 15 Bd2 Rxe1+ 16 Rxe1 c5 (Diagram 15)

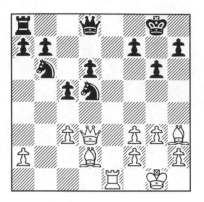

Diagram 15 (W)	Diagram 16 (W)
Ruling out Qd4 by White	The queenside pawns will advance

17 f4 Qf6 18 c4 Nb4 19 Qf3 Nc2 20 Rd1 Qe7 21 Qd3 Nb4 22 Bxb4

This gets the pawn back but now White faces a bad endgame. White's kingside pawn majority is stymied and he has weaknesses on the queenside.

22...cxb4 23 Qxd6 Qxd6 24 Rxd6 Re8 25 Bf1 Rc8 26 f5 gxf5 27 Kg2 Kf8

Improving his king before cashing in by taking the c4-pawn.

28 Bd3 Ke7 (Diagram 16) 29 Rh6

29 Rd4 Rc5 would leave White very passive, while Black would be ready to advance his queenside pawns.

29...Nxc4 30 Bxf5 Rd8 31 Rxh7

31 Rh4 b5 32 Bxh7 Rd2 is also good for Black.

31...Rd2 32 Kf3 Rxa2 33 h4 b3 34 h5 Kf6 35 g4 Ra5 0-1

White's h-pawn can be stopped, whereas Black's pawns on the queenside most definitely cannot.

Game 47
☐ **V.Mikhalevski** ■ **N.Davies**
Rishon LeZion 1995

---

1 d4 d6 2 Nf3 g6 3 c4 Bg4 4 Nc3 Bg7 5 e3 c5 6 dxc5 Bxc3+!

 WARNING: Remember that the immediate 6...dxc5 is bad, because of 7 Qxd8+ Kxd8 8 Bd2 followed by castling long.

7 bxc3 dxc5 8 Qxd8+ Kxd8 9 Ne5

The best try, though in any case White's shattered queenside pawns are going to be a problem in this endgame. J.Kraschl-Z.Kozul, Oberwart 1995, varied with 9 Nd2, but after 9...Nf6 10 a4 Nc6 11 a5 Kc7 12 Nb3 b6 13 f3 Bd7 14 e4 Rhb8 Black was doing well.

9...Be6 (Diagram 17)

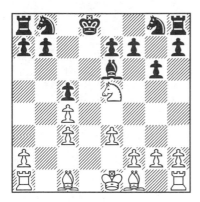

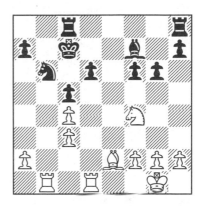

Diagram 17 (W)	Diagram 18 (B)
Already targeting c4	The c4-pawn will fall

10 e4

Aggression makes sense, as White should try to make something out of his bishop pair before he gets tied down to his weaknesses.

Here are two other possibilities:

a) 10 Be2 Nd7 11 Nxd7 was played in I.Hausner-V.Jansa, German League 1991, and now rather than 11...Bxd7 as in the game, 11...Kxd7 was probably best, keeping an eye on the c4-pawn. I think it's at least equal for Black.

b) 10 a4 Nd7 11 Nxd7 Kxd7! 12 a5 Nf6 13 f3 Ne8 14 Be2 Nd6 hit c4 with an excellent position in J.Ager-M.Ivanov, Arco 2002.

10...Nf6 11 Rb1 Nxe4 12 Rxb7 Nd6

Expelling the rook and hitting c4.

13 Rb1 Nd7 14 Bf4 Nb6 15 Be2 f6 16 Nd3 Rc8 17 Bxd6 exd6 18 Nf4 Bf7 19 0-0 Kc7 20 Rfd1 (Diagram 18)

White has done his best to make it difficult for Black to take on c4. Even so the pawn is falling.

20...Rb8 21 Rb3 Nxc4 22 Ra1 Rhe8 23 Bf3 Nd2 24 Ra3 Nxf3+ 25 gxf3 Rb7 (Diagram 19)

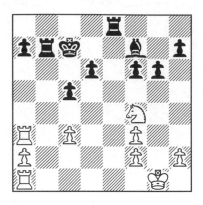

Diagram 19 (W)

Black is a pawn up

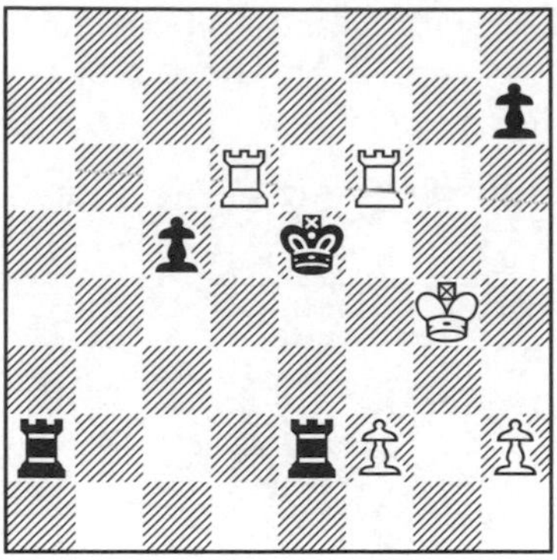

Diagram 20 (B)

Black to play and lose!

It's amazing that I should lose this. Black is a pawn up with the better position.

26 Rd1 g5 27 Nd5+ Bxd5 28 Rxd5 Kc6 29 Rd2 Ree7 30 Kg2 d5 31 f4 gxf4?!

Starting to let things slip. Either 31...h6 or 31...g4 would have been better.

32 Kf3 Rb6 33 Ra4 Rb1

And here 33...a6 was a better move. Now it's no longer clear that Black can win.

34 Rxf4 Re6 35 Ra4 Re7 36 Rf4 Re6 37 Ra4 Kb5

37...Re5 38 Rxa7 Rc1 was stronger, when Black still has something to play for.

38 Rxa7 Rc1 39 Rxd5 Rxc3+ 40 Kg4 Rc2 41 Rf5 Ree2 42 Rb7+ Kc6 43 Rf7 Rxa2 44 R5xf6+ Kd5 45 Rd7+ Ke5 46 Rdd6 (Diagram 20) 46...Re4+??

Having thrown away the win, I now throw away the draw. 46...h5+ 47 Kg5 Ke4 was the right way.

47 Kg5

Putting Black's king into a mating net. There's no good defence to 48 Rfe6 mate.

47...h6+ 48 Rxh6 1-0

Game 48
☐ **E.Gausel** ■ **V.Jansa**
Gausdal 1991

1 d4 d6 2 Nf3 g6 3 c4 Bg7 4 Nc3 Bg4 5 e3 c5 6 d5 Nf6 7 Be2

Another possibility is 7 h3, but Black has good play there too, for example 7...Bxf3 8 Qxf3 0-0 9 Qd1 Na6 10 Be2 Nc7 11 0-0 a6 12 Rb1 b5 13 b3 Rb8 14 Qc2 e6 15 dxe6 fxe6 16 e4 b4 17 Nd1 e5 18 Bg4 h5 19 Be2 Ne6 and the black knight was poised to land on d4 in S.Guliev-A.Kakageldyev, Simferopol 1989.

7...0-0 8 h3 Bxf3 9 Bxf3 Na6 10 0-0 Nc7 (Diagram 21)

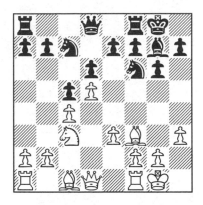

Diagram 21 (W)

Black plans ...b7-b5 or ...e7-e6

Diagram 22 (W)

The knight heads for d4

The knight is well placed here to support both ...b7-b5 and ...e7-e6.

11 Rb1

11 Bd2 was played against me by Paul Littlewood in the 1987 ARC Young Masters. In retrospect I would now prefer 11...Nd7 in this position, but the game went 11...Rb8 12 a4 b6 (12...e6!?) 13 Nb5 Rb7 14 Bc3 a6 15 Nxc7 Qxc7 16 Be2 e6 17 dxe6 fxe6 18 a5 with the better game for White.

11...Rb8 12 Be2 a6 13 a4 e5 14 dxe6

Trying to open the position for his bishops, but Black is always going to be doing well with this kind of central control. If instead 14 a5, Black could get counterplay with 14...Nd7 followed by ...f7-f5.

14...fxe6 15 e4 Qe7 16 Be3 Nd7 17 f4 Rbd8 18 Qd2 Nb8! (Diagram 22)

An instructive move from Jansa. The knight is heading towards its dream square on d4.

19 Bd3 Nc6 20 Rbe1 Bd4!

Another instructive move. Black can only occupy d4 with one of his minor pieces, and if this is to be his knight then the bishop on g7 will be redundant.

21 Bxd4 Nxd4 22 e5 d5 23 cxd5 exd5 24 Qf2

This might have been the time for White to recognize the latent problems in his position and head for simplification with 24 Ne2. After the game move Black starts to get the better of it.

24...Nce6 25 Qg3 Kh8 26 Rf2

26 Ne2 still looks like the right move. Now Black's queenside pawns surge forward.

26...c4 27 Bb1 b5 28 axb5 axb5 29 f5? (Diagram 23)

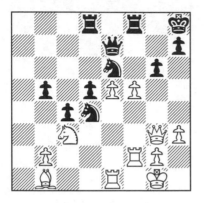

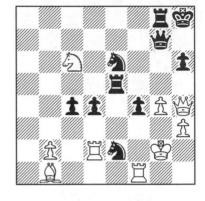

Diagram 23 (B)

White lashes out

Diagram 24 (B)

Black should win easily

Lashing out, but it never looks like enough for the pawn. Perhaps White was motivated by the mounting pressure and possibly Jansa's habitual time trouble. But it was better to bite the bullet with 29 Kh2.

29...gxf5 30 Ref1 f4 31 Qg4 Rg8 32 Qh5 Rg5 33 Qh6 Qg7 34 Qh4 b4 35 Na2 Rg8 36 g4 h6?!

Tying his own queen down to the defence of the h6-pawn definitely has the look of time trouble. Instead 36...h5 was better, when 37 Nxb4 can be met by 37...Qb7.

37 Nxb4 Rxe5 38 Rd2 Ne2+ 39 Kg2 d4 40 Nc6 (Diagram 24) 40...f3+?

On the final move before the time control Black fritters away his extra pawn. 40...Re3 would have kept him in the driving seat.

41 Rxf3 N6f4+?!

Another mistake. Black should play 41...N2f4+ 42 Kf1 Rh5 43 Qe7 Qxe7 44 Nxe7 Rxg4 45 hxg4 Rh1+ 46 Kf2 Rxb1 when the likely outcome is a draw. Now White is better... if he plays the right move.

42 Kf2?

42 Kf1! was correct, when Black is struggling after 42...Rh5 43 Qe7 Qxe7 44 Nxe7 Rxg4 45 Rxe2 etc.

42...Re6 43 Nxd4 Nxd4 44 Rxf4 Qe5 45 Re4 Rf8+ 46 Kg2 Nf3 47 Rxe5 Nxh4+ 48 Kg3 Rxe5 49 Kxh4 (Diagram 25)

Diagram 25 (B)

The game goes to and fro

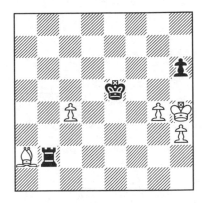

Diagram 26 (W)

Winning the bishop

So Black has emerged from the chaos with an extra exchange and problematic winning chances.

49...Rb8 50 Ba2 Rc5 51 Rc2 Rb4 52 Rd2?

An oversight. 52 Kg3 was stronger.

52...Kg7?

Missing a win with 52...Ra5 53 Bb1 c3. And this little routine is about to repeat itself.

53 Rd4? Kf6?

53...Rc7 54 Rd2 Ra7 55 Bb1 c3 is the same win as before.

54 b3?

54 Re4 leaves Black with nothing clear, but now Jansa pounces on his opportunity.

54...Ke5! 55 Rxc4 Rcxc4 56 bxc4 Rb2 (Diagram 26)

Winning the bishop, which White evidently missed when he played his 54th move. Now we finally get some smooth GM technique to bring home the bacon.

57 Kh5 Rxa2 58 Kxh6 Rh2 59 g5 Rxh3+ 60 Kg6 Rc3 0-1

Game 49
□ **H.Dobosz** ■ **V.Jansa**
Würzburg 1989

---

1 Nf3 g6 2 c4 Bg7 3 Nc3 d6 4 d4 Bg4 5 e3 c5 6 Be2 cxd4 7 Nxd4

One senses a distinct lack of ambition about this move; White seems to be avoiding imbalance against his higher rated adversary. But with most of the pieces still on the board a draw is not going to fall from the sky; White will have to work for it.

7...Bxe2 8 Ndxe2 Nf6 9 0-0 0-0 10 b3 (Diagram 27)

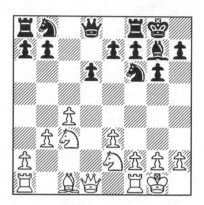

Diagram 27 (B)

Unambitious play by White

Diagram 28 (W)

Black controls the c-file

10...Nc6

There are two other playable moves here:

a) 10...d5 seems to equalize, but perhaps too cleanly for Jansa's purposes. P.Cramling-Z.Azmaiparashvili, Pamplona 1996, continued 11 cxd5 Nxd5 12 Qxd5 Qxd5 13 Nxd5 Bxa1 14 Ba3 Bg7 15 Nc7 Nc6 16 Nxa8 Rxa8 17 Rd1 Kf8 with equality.

b) 10...Nbd7 is probably a more flexible square for the knight, with a fighting game arising after 11 Bb2 a6 12 a3 Qc7 13 Rc1 e6 14 Nd4 Rac8 15 Qe2 Qb8 16 h3 Rfe8 in J.Diaz-M.Ginsburg, Las Vegas 2005. Given this position I might well put the knight on d7 myself, rather than adopt the more classical c6 development.

11 Bb2 Qa5 12 Qd2 a6 13 Rfd1 Rfc8

Putting pressure on the c-file.

14 Nd5 Nxd5 15 cxd5 Qxd2 16 Rxd2 Ne5 (Diagram 28)

It looks as if White's hoped for draw is getting closer, but Black is better in this position because of his control of the c-file. It's instructive to see how Jansa increases this advantage over the coming moves.

17 h3 Rc7 18 Rc1 Rxc1+ 19 Nxc1 Rc8 20 Ne2 f5!

Making it difficult for White to support d5 with another pawn, whilst preparing a route for Black's king to come in.

21 Kf1 Nd7 22 Bxg7 Kxg7 23 g4 Kf6 24 f3 Nb6 25 Kf2 Rc5 26 e4 fxe4 27 fxe4 Nd7 28 Rd3 Rc2 29 Rf3+ Kg7 (Diagram 29)

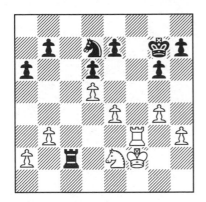

Diagram 29 (W)

Making steady progress

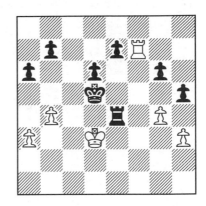

Diagram 30 (W)

Black is two pawns up

Black must bide his time as the immediate 29...Ke5 30 Ke3 Nc5 is answered by 31 Rf7. But he's making steady progress.

30 a3 Nc5 31 Re3 Kf6! 32 b4 Na4 33 Rd3

This time around 33 Rf3+ Ke5 34 Ke3 is answered by 34...Nc3.

33...Ke5 34 Ke3?!

Here 34 Re3 was a better try, but even so it looks good for Black after 34...Nb2 35 Rf3 Nc4 36 Rf7 Kxe4 37 Rxe7+ Ne5, threatening 38...Kd3.

34...Nb2 35 Rb3 Nc4+ 36 Kd3 Rd2+! 37 Kxc4 Rxe2 38 Rf3 Rxe4+ 39 Kd3 Kxd5 40 Rf7 h5 (Diagram 30)

With two extra pawns it's all over bar the shouting

41 Rg7 hxg4 42 hxg4 Re6 43 g5 Kc6 44 a4 d5 45 Kd4 Kd6 46 Rg8 Re4+ 47 Kc3 Re3+ 48 Kc2 Re6 49 Rb8 Kc7 50 Rg8 Rc6+ 51 Kd3 Rc4 52 Rg7 Kd7 53 b5 Rxa4 54 bxa6 Rxa6 55 Kd4 Kd6 56 Kc3 Ra3+ 57 Kc2 Rg3 58 Rxg6+ Ke5 59 Rb6 Rxg5 60 Rxb7 e6

Black won after a further 18 moves.

Game 50
☐ **L.Portisch** ■ **J.Timman**
Wijk aan Zee 1975

---

1 c4 g6 2 d4 Bg7 3 Nc3 d6 4 Nf3 Bg4 5 e3 c5!? 6 Be2 cxd4 7 exd4 Nh6!?

Again pursuing the plan of attacking d4 with great determination. The knight wants to jump to f5.

This game proves to be rather typical of this line: White's extra space and bishop pair are counterbalanced by Black's active minor pieces.

8 h3 Bxf3 9 Bxf3 (Diagram 31)

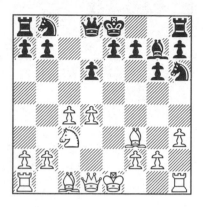
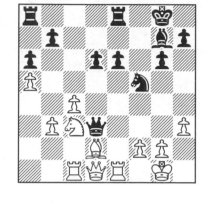

Diagram 31 (B)	**Diagram 32 (W)**
White threatens g2-g4	A mistake in judgement

With the idea of playing g2-g4 to shut the knight on h6 out of the game.

9...Nc6 10 d5 Ne5 11 Be2 Nf5 12 Bd2 0-0 13 0-0 a6 14 Re1 Qb6! 15 b3 Qd4 16 Rc1 Nd3 17 Bxd3 Qxd3 18 a4

18 g4? Bd4 19 Ne2 is bad because of 19...Nh4 20 Nf4 (20 Nxd4? Qxh3 is even worse) 20...Qf3 21 Qxf3 Nxf3+ winning the exchange.

18...Rfe8 19 a5 e6 20 dxe6 fxe6? (Diagram 32)

A mistake in judgement according to Timman, who said he should have recaptured on e6 with the rook, when White would no longer have Ne4 available.

The rest of the game is of little theoretical interest; it's a tough GM tussle which finally ends in a draw.

21 Ne4! Rac8 22 Bc3?

22 Bb4! would have been much stronger, for example 22...Qxd1 23 Rcxd1 d5 24 cxd5 exd5 25 Rxd5 Nd4 26 Bc5! Nxb3 27 Bb6 when Black can't challenge on the d-file and his b7-pawn is weak.

22...Qxd1 23 Rexd1 d5 24 cxd5 exd5 25 Bxg7 dxe4

Not 25...Rxc1?? because of 26 Nf6+, winning material.

26 Rxc8 Rxc8 27 Bf6 Kf7 28 Bg5 Ke6 29 g4 Nd6 30 Rd4 Ke5 31 Bf6+ Ke6 32 Bh4 Ke5 33 Rd1 Ke6 34 Rd4 Ke5 35 Bf6+ Ke6 36 g5?? (Diagram 33)

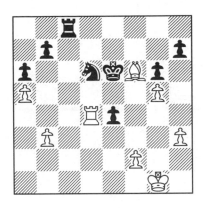

Diagram 33 (B)

Giving Black the f5-square

Diagram 34 (W)

Now Portisch hangs on

A positional blunder, giving Black the f5-square. 36 Bh4 was the right move with a likely draw, whereas now Black is in the driving seat.

36...Rc5 37 Bd8 Rd5 38 Rb4 Rb5 39 Rxb5 Nxb5 40 Bf6 Na7 41 f3 Kf5 42 fxe4+ Kxe4 43 Kg2 Nc6 44 Bc3 Kd3 45 Be1 Nd4 46 b4 Nc2 47 Bf2 Nxb4

47...Kc4! intending ...Kxb4 would have made it easier.

48 Kf3 Nc6 49 Be1 Kd4

And here 49...Nd4+ was better. Now White has survival chances.

50 Kf4 Kd5? (Diagram 34)

Black's last winning chance was with 50...Ne5, for example 51 Bf2+ Kd5 52 Bb6 Nc4 53 Bd8 Kd6 54 Ke4 Kd7 55 Kd4 Nd2! and a knight fork picks up another pawn. After the game move Portisch hangs onto a draw with brilliant defence.

51 h4! Ne5 52 Bc3 Nc4 53 h5 b6 54 axb6 Nxb6 55 hxg6 hxg6 56 Ke3 Nc4+ 57 Kd3 Ne5+ 58 Kc2 Nf3 59 Bf6 Ke6 60 Kc3 Kf5 61 Kb4 Nxg5 62 Be7 Ne4 63 Bh4! Ke6 64 Ka5 Nc5 65 Kb6 Kd6 66 Bg3+ Kd5 67 Bh4 Kc4 68 Ka5 Kd4 69 Kb6 Kd5 70 Be7 Kc4 71 Bh4 Kb4 72 Be1+ ½-½

Summary

In the Lesser Averbakh White still tries to take space but hopes to avoid the weakening of d4 by delaying or omitting e2-e4. The problem is that 4 Nf3 is also a committal move, in that it allows Black to play 4...Bg4. The positions that arise after 5 e3 c5!? then seem fine for Black, whichever way the central tension is resolved.

Chapter Ten

Other 1 d4 Lines

■ **Introduction**

■ **Illustrative Games**

Introduction

One of the strengths of the Modern Defence is it's efficacy against the sort of Queen's Pawn Openings, such as the Torre Attack, London and Colle Systems, which are very popular at club level. Black can mess White up early on and stop him getting the sort of automated attack that makes these lines so dangerous in practice.

1 d4 g6 2 Nf3 Bg7 (Diagram 1)

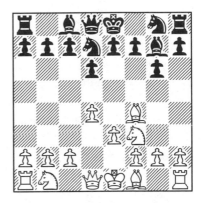

Diagram 1 (W)

White has numerous options

Diagram 2 (W)

Achieving ...e7-e5 with ease

3 g3

White's other Queen's Pawn options are:

a) 3 Bg5 attempts to set up a Torre Attack but leaves White's queenside vulnerable to a dark square counterattack. Black can play 3...c5!, after which 4 e3 cxd4 5 exd4 Nf6 followed by 6...0-0 and 7...d6 gives him a sound and flexible position. Ambitious players might also care to examine the consequences of a sharp move such as 4...Qb6!?.

b) 3 Bf4 (the London System) makes nowhere near as much sense here as it would if a knight were already on f6. The point is that Black finds it that much easier to achieve ...e7-e5, which wins time against the bishop on f4; for example 3...d6 4 e3 Nd7 **(Diagram 2)** 5 Bc4 (5 h3 e5 6 Bh2 exd4 7 exd4 Ne7 is examined in Game 52, Kozak-Vokac) 5...e5 6 dxe5 dxe5 and now 7 Bxf7+? Kxf7 8 Ng5+ Ke7 9 Qd5 Nh6 10 Qe6+ Kf8 proved to be unsound in Koch-Nunn, Wiesbaden 1981 (see Game 51).

c) 3 e3, aiming for a Colle, is not very scary. Black could get ambitious now with 3...f5 followed by 4...Nf6, angling for a Leningrad Dutch set-up in which White's 3 e3 doesn't make much sense. Personally I have tended to adopt a King's Indian set-up with 3...Nf6 followed by 4...0-0, 5...d6, 6...Nbd7 and 7...e5 and achieved more than satisfactory results.

d) 3 c3 is a semi-waiting move, after which 3...d6 4 Bf4 returns to line "b" above, and 4 e4 transposes into Geller's System in Chapter Six. Should White play 4 Bg5 (avoiding the dangers of 3 Bg5 c5!) Black can again adopt a good Leningrad Dutch set-up with 4...h6 5 Bh4 f5. This makes 3 c3 look like an inefficient use of time and White's bishop on h4 seems rather ineffective.

3...d5

An idea I've used in my own games is 3...c5 and, after 4 c3, to play 4...Qa5!?, threatening to whittle away White's centre pawns with 5...cxd4 because White's own c-pawn is pinned. R.Simic-N.Davies, Vrnjacka Banja 1991, continued 5 Bg2 cxd4 6 Nxd4 Nf6 7 0-0 0-0 8 e4 Nc6 9 h3 d6 10 Be3 Bd7 11 Nd2 whereupon the players boldly agreed to a draw. This was a very peaceful tournament and Black has achieved full equality.

The reason I'm not giving this line here is that 4 d5 is probably better for White due to his extra space. Of course it is also double-edged, so ambitious players may want to try Black.

4 Bg2 Nh6!? (Diagram 3)

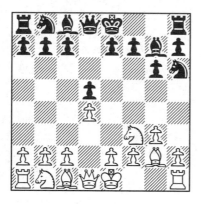
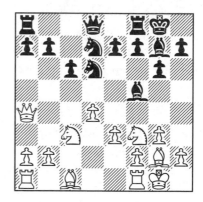

Diagram 3 (W)

A very interesting move

Diagram 4 (W)

Black has excellent prospects

Black places the knight where it doesn't impede the action of the bishop on g7, whilst introducing the possibility of putting the knight on f5. Obviously this applies far more pressure to the d4-pawn than had the knight hopped out to f6.

5 c4?!

This helps Black because it weakens d4, but if a player of Polugaevsky's class makes such an error then so can everyone else. There are a couple of alternatives:

a) 5 c3 Nf5 6 Nbd2 (or 5 Nbd2 Nf5 6 c3) 6...Nd6 discouraged both c3-d4 and e2-e4, and after 7 h4?! c6 8 h5 Bf5 9 Nb3 Nd7 10 Nh4 Be6 11 f3 Bf6 Black was already better in P.Nikolic-S.Agdestein, Reykjavik 1996.

b) 5 0-0 0-0 6 c3 c6 7 Nbd2 f5!? 8 Ne5 Nd7 9 Nd3 Nf7 10 Nf3 e5 left Black with more space in G.Barcza-A.Bisguier, Stockholm Interzonal 1962.

5...dxc4 6 Qa4+

Black would also take the initiative after 6 Na3 Nf5 7 e3 c5!.

6...c6 7 Qxc4 Nf5 8 e3 Nd6!

Hitting the queen and controlling e4

9 Qa4 Bf5 10 0-0 0-0 11 Nc3 Nd7 (Diagram 4)

and Black's active pieces gave him excellent prospects in Polugaevsky-Romanishin, USSR Championship 1977 (see Game 53).

Illustrative Games

Game 51
☐ **R.Koch** ■ **J.Nunn**
Wiesbaden 1981

1 d4 g6 2 Nf3 Bg7 3 Bf4 d6 4 e3 Nd7 5 Bc4 e5 6 dxe5 dxe5 7 Bxf7+? (Diagram 5)

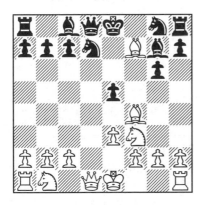
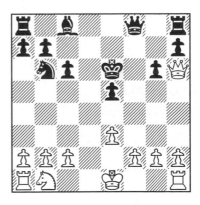

Diagram 5 (B)	Diagram 6 (W)
An incorrect sacrifice	Black remains a piece up

This doesn't work, though it does cause Black some anxious moments.

 WARNING: Black should always be on the lookout for Bc4xf7+ ideas.

White should play 7 Bg5, despite the fact that it loses a tempo whilst all Black's moves have been useful. After 7...Ngf6 8 Nc3 h6 9 Bh4 (9 Bxf6 Qxf6 10 h4 Nb6 11 Nd5 Nxd5 12 Qxd5 0-0 13 h5 c6 14 Qa5 e4 15 Nd4 b6 16 Qa3 gxh5 17 c3 Bg4 18 Be2 c5 19 Nb3 Rfd8 was good for Black in J.Bellon Lopez-V.Bologan, Gibraltar 2006) 9...0-0 10 Nd5 g5 11 Nxf6+ Qxf6 12 Bg3 e4 13 Nd2 Nb6 14 Nxe4 Qe7 15 Nd2 Nxc4 16 Nxc4 Qb4+ 17 Nd2 Be6 Black recovered the pawn with an excellent game in R.Ferry-J.Seret, Meribel 1998.

7...Kxf7 8 Ng5+ Ke7 9 Qd5 Nh6

And not 9...exf4?? because of 10 Qe6+ Kf8 11 Qf7 mate.

10 Qe6+

After 10 Bg3 Nb6 White would have nothing.

10...Kf8 11 Qd5 c6 12 Ne6+ Ke7 13 Bg5+ Bf6 14 Qc4 Nb6 15 Bxf6+ Kxf6 16 Qh4+ Kxe6 17 Qxh6 Qf8 (Diagram 6)

The smoke is starting to clear and White only has a pawn for his sacrificed piece.

18 Qh4 Qe7 19 Qe4 Nd5 20 0-0 Kf7 21 Nd2 Kg7 22 c4 Bf5 23 Qf3 Nf6

With Black's king also reaching safety this would have been a reasonable place for White to throw in the towel. Instead he fights on and on...

24 e4 Rhd8 25 Qe3 Be6 26 Qc3 Rd4 27 f4 Rad8 28 fxe5 Ng4 29 Nb3 Rxc4

29...Rd3 30 Qc2 Qg5 was also good. The main danger in having such positions as Black is boredom.

30 Qg3 Rxe4 31 Rae1 Rxe1 32 Rxe1 Qb4 33 h3 Rd3! 34 Qh4 Qb6+ 35 Kh1 Rxh3+! 0-1

White has finally had enough. If he takes on h3 with the pawn then 36...Bd5+ leads to mate, and if he takes with the queen then 36...Nf2+ follows.

Game 52
☐ **M.Kozak** ■ **M.Vokac**
Czech League 1996

---

1 Nf3 g6 2 d4 Bg7 3 Bf4 d6 4 e3 Nd7 5 h3 (Diagram 7)

The idea behind this move is to combine the presence of the bishop on the h2-b8 diagonal with an advance of White's c-pawn, a strategy which was beautifully realized in B.Spassky-E.Bukic, Bugojno 1978: 1 d4 Nf6 2 Nf3 g6 3 Bf4 Bg7 4 e3 0-0 5 Be2 d6 6 0-0 Nbd7 7 h3 Qe8 8 c4 e5 9 Bh2 Qe7 10 Nc3 e4 11 Nd2 Re8 12 Nb5 Qd8 13 c5 **(Diagram 8)** 13...a6 14 cxd6 axb5 15 dxc7 Qe7 16 Bxb5 Bf8 17 Nc4 Qe6 18 Qc2 Qd5 19 a4 Re6 20 Rfc1 Ne8 21 Qc3 Nef6 22 Ne5 Nb6 23 Nc4 Nfd7 24 Qb3 Rf6 25 Bxd7 Nxd7 26 Qb5 Qf5 27 Bg3 Rfa6 28 d5 Qf6 29 a5 h5 30 b4 h4 31 Bh2 Qf5 32 Rf1 g5 33 f3 Rg6 34 Rad1 exf3 35 Rxf3 Qc2 36 Rd2 Qc3 37 d6 Ra6 38 e4 Qc1+ 39 Rf1 Qc3 40 Qd5 Nf6 41 Rxf6 1-0. This is what White wants, but without Black's knight committed to f6 things are very different.

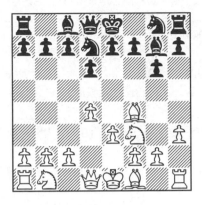

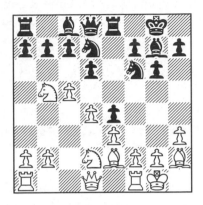

Diagram 7 (B)

Making a home for the bishop

Diagram 8 (B)

Powering up the h2-b8 diagonal

5...e5 6 Bh2 exd4 (Diagram 9)

Rather than lunge forward with ...e5-e4 (along the lines of Spassky-Bukic) Black simply exchanges. After this the bishop on h2 is not particularly well placed.

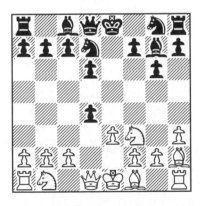

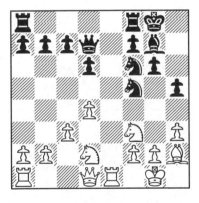

Diagram 9 (W)

The simplest solution

Diagram 10 (W)

Safeguarding the f5-outpost

7 exd4 Ne7

 TIP: Always consider 'creative' developments of the king's knight in the Modern, rather than just plonking it out on f6.

8 Bd3 0-0 9 0-0 Nf6 10 Nbd2

Another example is H.Kreindl-R.Lau, Aschach 2002, which went 10 Re1 Bf5 11 Nh4 Bxd3 12 Qxd3 Qd7 13 Nd2 b5 14 Re2 Ned5 15 c3 Rfe8 16 Rae1 Rxe2 17 Rxe2 a5 18 Ne4 Qc6 19 Nxf6+ Bxf6 and Black had built up an advantage on the queenside.

10...Bf5 11 Bxf5 Nxf5 12 Re1 Qd7 13 c3 h5 (Diagram 10)

Not so much an attacking gesture as simple support for the knight on f5. Black is inhibiting g2-g4.

14 Ne4 Nxe4 15 Rxe4 Rae8 16 Qd3 Rxe4 17 Qxe4 Qb5 18 Qc2 Re8 19 Re1 Rxe1+ 20 Nxe1 Qe8 21 Kf1 Qe6

Black is a tiny bit better here, though a long way from actually winning the game. He is helped by being the stronger player.

22 Qb3 Qe4 23 Qc2 Qe6 24 Qb3 Qe4 25 Qc2 Qc6

Twofold repetitions are a useful means of psychological torture.

26 Qe2 Bh6 27 Nd3 a5 28 Bf4? (Diagram 11)

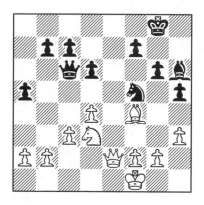

Diagram 11 (B)

An oversight by White

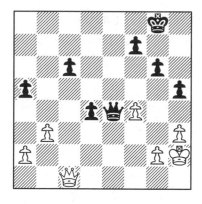

Diagram 12 (W)

Black is winning the queen endgame

28 Ne1 was better, when Black would presumably have continued gaining space with 28...a4.

28...Nxd4! 29 cxd4 Bxf4 30 d5

If 30 Nxf4 Qc1+ picks up the knight and leaves Black with an extra pawn in the queen endgame.

30...Qc4 31 b3 Qd4 32 Nxf4 Qxf4 33 Qc2 Qd4 34 Kg1 Qc5 35 Qd2 c6 36 dxc6 bxc6 37 Kh2 d5 38 f4 Qb4 39 Qe3 Qe4 40 Qc1 d4 (Diagram 12)

Two of the major factors in queen endgames are passed pawns and having a safer king. In this example Black's position ticks both of these boxes.

41 Kg3 Qe2 42 Qxc6 Qe3+ 43 Kh2 Qxf4+ 44 g3 Qe5 45 Qf3 h4 46 Kg2 Qxg3+

Liquidating into a winning pawn endgame. A passed white b-pawn can easily be stopped by Black's king.

47 Qxg3 hxg3 48 Kxg3 Kf8 49 Kf3 f5 50 h4 Ke7 51 a3 Kd6 52 Kf4 Kd5 53 Kf3 Ke5 54 Kf2 Ke4 55 Ke2 f4 0-1

Game 53
☐ **L.Polugaevsky** ■ **O.Romanishin**
USSR Championship, Leningrad 1977

---

1 Nf3 g6 2 d4 Bg7 3 g3 d5 4 Bg2 Nh6!? 5 c4?! (Diagram 13)

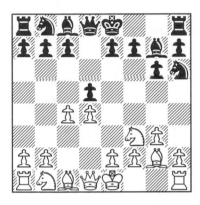
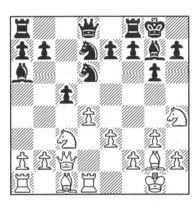

Diagram 13 (B)	**Diagram 14 (W)**
Probably a mistake	Black seizes the initiative

As I mentioned in the introduction, this natural move is probably a mistake. White should choose between 5 c3, 5 0-0 and 5 Nbd2.

5...dxc4 6 Qa4+

White can also recover the pawn with 6 Na3, but then 6...Nf5 7 e3 c5 takes the initiative.

6...c6 7 Qxc4 Nf5 8 e3 Nd6! 9 Qa4

Black can meet 9 Qe2 with 9...b6, threatening 10...Ba6, though this might have been White's best chance after 10 Ne5!?.

9...Bf5 10 0-0 0-0 11 Nc3 Nd7 12 Nh4 Bd3

Transferring the bishop to a better diagonal.

13 Rd1 Ba6 14 Qc2

14 e4 looks like an improvement, with approximate equality after 14...c5 15 dxc5 Nxc5 16 Qc2 Ne6. Now Black seizes the initiative.

14...c5! (Diagram 14) 15 Nf3 Rc8 16 d5 b5 17 e4

A preliminary 17 a3 could also be considered.

17...b4 18 Ne2 Nc4! 19 Bh3! Rb8

Black can repeat the position with 19...Na3 20 Qd2 Nc4 21 Qc2 Na3, but evidently he wants more.

20 Rb1 Nce5 21 Ne1 Qb6!

On 21...Qa5 Polu was intending 22 f4! Qxa2 23 fxe5 b3 24 Qd2 Qxb1, after which 25 Nc3! (25 Bxd7 Qxe4 is good for Black) 25...Qa1 26 Bxd7 Bxe5 27 Nf3 leaves Black without enough compensation.

22 Be3

Now 22 f4 b3 23 axb3 c4+ 24 Kh1 (or 24 Nd4 Nd3) 24...cxb3 25 Qc3 Nd3 is just good for Black.

22...Qb5 23 Nc1! Rfc8? (Diagram 15)

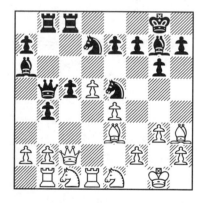

Diagram 15 (W)

Pinning his own knight

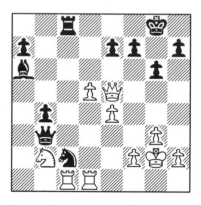

Diagram 16 (B)

Renewed complications

Black should have preferred 23...Rfd8.

24 Ncd3! c4?!

Intending the following exchange sacrifice, but after White's 27th he gets insufficient compensation.

25 Nxe5 Nxe5 26 Bxc8 Rxc8 27 a4! Qd7 28 Bd4 c3 29 Kg2!

White needs to watch his step as 29 bxc3?? runs into 29...Qh3!.

29...Nc4 30 Bxg7 Kxg7 31 Nd3 cxb2 32 Qe2 Qxa4 33 Nxb2 Qa2 34 Qd3! Kg8 35

Qd4?

35 Nxc4! Bxc4 36 Qd4 was the right way. Now Black manages to bring about renewed complications.

35...Na3! 36 Ra1 Qb3 37 Rac1 Nc2 38 Qe5 (Diagram 16) 38...Be2?

Black might do better to exchange queens first with 38...Qc3 39 Qxc3 (not 39 Qxe7? Ne3+ 40 fxe3 Qxb2+) 39...Rxc3 and then 40...Be2, or if 40 e5 there follows 40...Kf8 41 d6 exd6 42 exd6 Ke8.

39 Rd2 Bf3+ 40 Kg1 a5?

Polugaevsky's suggestion of 40...Rc3? would have been refuted by 41 d6! exd6 42 Rxd6, exploiting the weakness of Black's back rank. Instead, 40...Qa2 was relatively best, though 41 d6 exd6 42 Rxd6 still looks good for White.

41 Rd3 Rc3 42 Qb8+

Missing a brilliant win with 42 d6!! Qxb2 43 Rf1! and if 43...Nd4 (or 43...exd6 44 Rxd6) 44 Qxd4! exd6 45 Rxf3 etc.

42...Kg7 43 Qe5+ Kh6

43...Kg8? would give White another chance to find 44 d6!! etc.

44 Rxc3 Qxc3

44...bxc3 45 Nd3 is a lot easier.

45 Qxc3 bxc3 46 Na4 Bxe4 47 Nxc3 Bd3 48 Rb1! (Diagram 17)

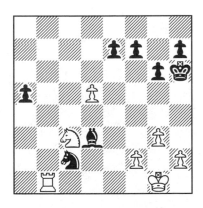

Diagram 17 (B)

White has consolidated

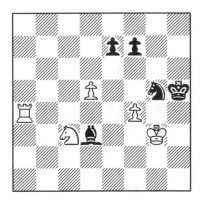

Diagram 18 (B)

Ra4-a7 will follow

48...Kg5

Black can eliminate the d-pawn with 48...Bc4 49 Rb7 Nb4 50 Rxe7 Nxd5, but after 51 Nxd5 Bxd5 52 Re5 Be6 53 Rxa5 Kg7 54 f4 the position is a technical win for

White.

49 Rb7 Kf6 50 Ra7 Nd4 51 Rxa5

The preliminary 51 f4! is better. Even so White is winning.

51...Nf3+ 52 Kg2 Ne1+ 53 Kh1 g5 54 Ra4! Nf3 55 h4! h6 56 Kg2 Ne1+ 57 Kh3 Kg6

Or if 57...Bf1+ 58 Kg4 Kg6 there follows 59 h5+ Kf6 60 Ra1 etc.

58 g4 h5 59 hxg5 Nf3 60 gxh5+ Kxh5 61 Kg3 Nxg5 62 f4 1-0 (Diagram 18)

After the knight retreats White wins with 63 Ra7.

This game was more a demonstration of Polugaevsky's playing strength than the merits of his opening. Black obtained very good counterplay early on.

Summary

One of the great advantages of the Modern at club level is that many perennial favourites such as the Torre, Colle and London System have very little bite. By delaying the development of his king's knight, Black maintains great flexibility in his set-up. He might send the knight to f5 via h6, or perhaps play ...f7-f5, while against Bf4 he can achieve ...e7-e5 far more quickly than in the analogous King's Indian positions, since the unobstructed g7-bishop covers the e5-square.

White's most important line in this chapter involves 2 Nf3 and 3 g3, but here too Black can mix it, either with Romanishin's recipe against Polugaevsky in Game 53, or indeed 3...c5. Once again there are no safe options for White.

Chapter Eleven

Flank Openings

Introduction

Illustrative Games

Introduction

A common trend amongst players who wish to "avoid theory" is to adopt flank openings, and I myself have frequently opened with 1 Nf3, 1 c4 or 1 g3 in order to put my opponent more on his own resources. The drawback with such methods is that they allow Black far more scope. In the Modern Defence, after playing 1...g6 and 2...Bg7, Black can stake a claim for the middle of the board with 3...e5, after which transposition into a reversed Closed Sicilian is likely.

1 c4

If White adopts a King's Indian Attack set-up with 1 Nf3 g6 2 g3 Bg7 3 Bg2 Black can take the centre with 3...e5 **(Diagram 1)**.

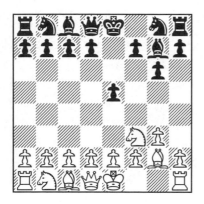

Diagram 1 (W)

Black takes the centre

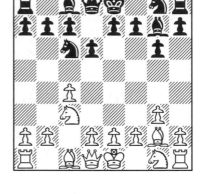

Diagram 2 (W)

A major junction

Then 4 d3 Nc6 5 c4 will probably transpose into the main line. The reciprocal 4 e4, on the other hand, would grant Black rather good prospects because White has blocked the advance of his f-pawn with his knight. Barcza-Tal, Havana 1963, continued 4...Nc6 5 0-0 d6 6 Nc3 Nge7 7 Nd5 0-0 8 Nxe7+ Qxe7 9 c3 f5 10 exf5 e4 11 Ne1 Bxf5 with an excellent position for Black (see Game 54).

1...g6 2 Nc3 Bg7 3 g3 Nc6 4 Bg2 d6 (Diagram 2)

This is a major junction, at which White can choose between a variety of set-ups.

5 Nf3

Apart from the text (which may have already been played as early as move one), the two most popular plans are Botvinnik's 5 e4 and the quieter 5 e3, but White can also prepare a queenside expansion with 5 Rb1, or play the semi-waiting move 5 d3.

a) 5 e4 was well met in Benko-Botvinnik (Game 55) by 5...e5 6 d3 Nge7 7 Nge2 Be6 8 Nd5 0-0 9 0-0 Qd7 10 Be3 f5 11 Qd2 Rf7 12 Rae1 Raf8 13 f4 fxe4 14 dxe4 Nc8 15 c5 Bh3, undermining the support for White's e4-pawn by trading off his light-squared bishop.

b) After 5 e3 I don't like plans based on an early ...f7-f5 so much, because White's set-up (with 6 Nge2) will make it well-nigh impossible for Black to play ...f5-f4 to release his light-squared bishop. I much prefer the plan of 5...e5 6 Nge2 h5 used in Game 56 (Sunye Neto-Nunn).

c) 5 d3 e5 6 Rb1 allows Black to regroup with 6...Be6 7 b4 Qd7, when 8 b5 can be answered by 8...Nd8, protecting the b7-pawn.

d) 5 Rb1 tries to avoid the ...Be6 and ...Qd7 regrouping, as after 5...e5 6 b4 Be6 7 b5 the d8-square is not yet available for the knight. But Black can move his bishop one square further with 6...Bf5!, after which 7 d3 Qd7 clears d8 in time. R.Hartoch-F.Gheorghiu, Amsterdam 1969, continued 8 e3 Nge7 9 h3 0-0 10 Nge2 h6 11 Nd5 Nd8 12 Nxe7+ Qxe7 13 0-0 Qd7 14 Kh2 Be6 15 Nc3 f5 16 Qb3 Qf7 17 Rd1 e4 and Black had obtained counterplay against c4.

5...e5 6 d3 f5 7 0-0 Nf6 (Diagram 3)

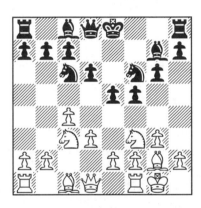

Diagram 3 (W)
White must decide on a plan

Diagram 4 (B)
Should Black castle here?

8 Rb1

The traditional and most logical plan for White is the advance of his b-pawn, but a couple of other ideas have been tried.

In B.Wagner-E.Prie, Strasbourg 1991, White tried to block the further advance of Black's f-pawn with 8 Ne1 0-0 9 f4, but after 9...exf4 10 Bxf4 Nh5 11 Bd2 Ne5 12 Nf3 c6 13 Qc2 f4 14 gxf4 Nxf4 15 Bxf4 Rxf4 16 e3 Nxf3+ 17 Bxf3 Rf8 18 Kh1 Qe7 19 Qe2 Bd7 20 Rae1 Rae8 21 d4 Bh3 22 Rg1 Qh4 23 Qd1 Qf2 24 Rg3 the game arrives at Test Position 29.

Another possibility is 8 Nd5, after which Berkovich-Davies, Tel Aviv 1992, continued 8...0-0 9 Bg5 Ne7 10 Nxf6+ Bxf6 11 Bxf6 Rxf6 12 c5 Nc6 13 cxd6 cxd6 with a comfortable position for Black (see Game 57).

8...h6

Cutting out the possibility of Bc1-g5 whilst furthering his kingside aims. Having said that, the immediate 8...0-0 is also eminently playable.

9 b4 (Diagram 4) 9...0-0

Black omitted castling altogether in the interesting game J.Sunye Neto-L.Hazai, Tuzla 1983, winning in dramatic style after 9...g5!? 10 Qb3 Be6 11 b5 Ne7 12 Ne1 Qc8 13 a4 f4 14 Ba3 h5 15 Nf3 h4 16 Nxg5 hxg3 17 fxg3 Ng4 18 Nd5 Bxd5 19 cxd5 Rxh2 20 Ne6 Kf7 21 d4 Qh8 22 Qf3 Rh1+ 0-1.

Another idea is to delay White's queenside advance with 9...a6, an example of this plan being the game I.Johannsson-A.J.Mestel, Lucerne Olympiad 1982, which reached Test Position 30 after 10 Bd2 0-0 (in truth Black played 8...0-0 and 10...h6) 11 a4 Be6 12 Ne1 Rb8 13 b5 axb5 14 axb5 Ne7 15 Nc2 g5 16 Ra1 f4 17 Ra7 b6 18 Nb4 Rc8 19 Qc2 Nf5 20 Nc6 Qe8 21 e3 Kh8 22 Ne4 Nxe4 23 Bxe4 f3 24 Bxf5 Bxf5 25 e4 Qh5 26 Kh1 Bh3 27 Rfa1 Bg2+ 28 Kg1.

10 b5

In A.Ledger-N.Davies, London Lloyds Bank 1991, my opponent played to open the c-file with 10 Nd2 g5 11 Nd5 Nxd5 12 cxd5, but it is not a particularly difficult task to defend just one square (i.e. c7), and the drawback of this plan for White is that it reduces the influence of his bishop on g2. The game went on 12...Ne7 13 Nc4 Ng6 14 Qc2 Rf7 15 a4 h5 16 b5 b6 17 a5 Bd7 18 Bd2 h4 19 Rfc1 Qf6 20 Rb4 Raf8 21 Be1 Bh6 22 Ra1 hxg3 23 hxg3 Kh8 24 axb6 axb6 25 Ra7 Nf4! 26 Rxc7 Nxg2 27 Kxg2 f4 28 Nd2? Qf5 29 Rxd7 Rxd7 30 f3 g4! 31 Rc4 Rh7 32 Rc7 Bg7 33 gxf4 exf4 34 d4 Qh5 0-1.

10...Ne7 11 a4 (Diagram 5)

11 Nd2 would be answered by 11...g5 as in Ledger-Davies above.

11...Be6!

I must reluctantly admit that this finesse is probably best, despite having played it differently in one of my own games. In E.Brestian-N.Davies, Gausdal 1992, I played the immediate 11...g5, the drawback of which is that White can answer with 12 c5. Even so this position is highly complex and fully playable, the sequel being 12...Ng6 13 cxd6 cxd6 14 Ba3 Be6 15 Nd2 Rf7 16 Nb3 Rc8 17 Bb4 Rfc7 18 Qd2 d5 19 d4 e4 20 a5 b6 21 axb6 axb6 22 Rfc1 Qd7 23 Ba3 Rc4 24 Nd1 f4 with the better game for Black.

12 Ba3

12 c5? is now met by 12...dxc5 13 Nxe5 Ne8!, skewering the knights on e5 and c3.

12...Rc8!

The immediate 12...b6? is bad because of 13 Nxe5!.

13 Nd2 b6 (Diagram 6)

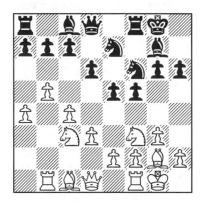

Diagram 5 (B)	**Diagram 6 (W)**
White plans c4-c5	Black is ready to attack

Black has defended his queenside and is ready to pursue the initiative on the opposite flank. The instructive game Psakhis-Kasparov, La Manga 1990, ended in a famous victory for Black (see Game 58).

Illustrative Games

Game 54
☐ **G.Barcza** ■ **M.Tal**
Havana 1963

1 Nf3 g6 2 g3 Bg7 3 Bg2 e5 4 e4 (Diagram 7)

The drawback with White's position is that his knight on f3 blocks the advance of his f-pawn. Black is careful not to do the same, as f2-f4 by White and ...f7-f5 by Black are the key pawn levers in this kind of position.

4...Nc6 5 0-0 d6 6 Nc3

Another and perhaps superior possibility is 6 c3, when L.Kavalek-M.Stean, Montilla 1977, continued 6...Nh6 (6...Nge7 7 d4 Bg4 may be better, as after 8 Qb3 exd4 9 Qxb7 Black's knight on c6 is already protected) 7 d4 f6 (7...Bg4!? is another possibility, trying to get White to close the centre with 8 d5 and then counterattack with ...f7-f5 later on; 8 Qb3 may be the critical response) 8 Qb3 Nf7 9 Na3 0-0 10 Be3

Qe7 11 Rfe1 Ncd8 12 Rad1 Ne6 13 Nc4 Re8 14 Bc1 Nf8 15 Ne3 c6 16 h4 Qc7 with Black setting up a solid, if somewhat convoluted defence.

6...Nge7 (Diagram 8)

 NOTE: It's worth repeating that Black doesn't block his f-pawn with this move. He's playing for ...f7-f5.

7 Nd5

7 d3 0-0 would leave Black ready to play ...f7-f5, for example 8 Be3 f5 9 Qd2 Nd4 10 Bg5 Ne6 11 Nd5 Nxg5 12 Qxg5 Nxd5 13 Qxd8 Rxd8 14 exd5 Bf6 gave Black a nice two bishop endgame in N.Borge-M.Petursson, Stockholm 1991.

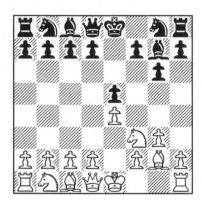

Diagram 7 (B)	Diagram 8 (W)
White's f-pawn is blocked	Black keeps his f-pawn free

7...0-0 8 Nxe7+ Qxe7 9 c3 f5 10 exf5 e4 11 Ne1

11 Re1 might have been a better move, but Tal's opponents usually showed a great reluctance to undefend squares like f7 or f2. One possibility for Black would then be 11...Qf6, after which 12 Rxe4 Bxf5 13 Re1? is bad because of 13...Bg4 (note the weakness of f2!).

11...Bxf5 12 d4 Qd7 13 f3 d5 14 fxe4 Bxe4 15 Rxf8+ Rxf8 16 Bxe4 dxe4 (Diagram 9)

The exchange of light-squared bishops has left White's king very weak, which prompts him to liquidate into an inferior endgame.

17 Qe2 Qe6 18 Nc2 Ne7 19 Ne3 Rf3 20 Qc4?!

20 Bd2 was preferable. Barcza no doubt wanted to clip the wings of the young 'Wizard from Riga', but discovers that his opponent isn't too bad in endgames either.

20...Qxc4 21 Nxc4 Nd5 22 Kg2?!

White should probably play 22 Nd2, but even then Black has some pressure after 22...Re3 23 Kf2 b5 24 Nb3 Rf3+ 25 Ke2 Bf8.

22...Rd3 23 Bf4?! (Diagram 10) 23...b5 24 Ne5 Nxf4+ 25 gxf4 Rd2+ 26 Kg3 Rxb2 27 a4 b4 28 cxb4 Rb3+?!

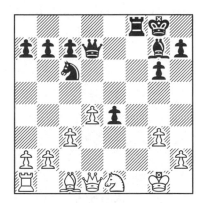

Diagram 9 (W)	Diagram 10 (B)
White is weak on the light squares	Bad, but then what else?

28...Rxb4 looks simpler here, just going for a harvest of pawns.

29 Kf2 Bh6 30 Re1 Bxf4 31 Rxe4 Bxh2 32 Nc6 a6 33 Re8+ Kg7 34 Ra8 h5 35 Rxa6 Bg3+ 36 Kg2 h4 37 Kh3 Be1+ 38 Kh2 h3 39 Na5 Rxb4 40 Re6??

On the last move before the time control Barcza loses his knight. 40 Ra7 would have been more tenacious.

40...Rb2+ 41 Kxh3 Bxa5 42 Ra6 Bb6 43 d5 Rd2 44 a5 Bc5 45 Rc6 Bd6 0-1

Game 55
□ **P.Benko** ■ **M.Botvinnik**
Monte Carlo 1968

---

1 c4 g6 2 g3 Bg7 3 Bg2 e5 4 Nc3 Ne7 5 e4 (Diagram 11)

The Botvinnik System, but with Botvinnik playing against it!

5...d6 6 Nge2 Nbc6 7 d3 f5

"Careful play characteristic of an experienced Grandmaster," noted Botvinnik, concerned that early castling might be answered by h2-h4.

8 Nd5 0-0 9 Be3 Be6 10 Qd2 Qd7 11 0-0 Rf7 12 Rae1 Raf8 13 f4 (Diagram 12)

While this is the typical break in such position, the problem with it here is that it weakens e4, although it requires masterful play by Black to exploit this factor.

Subsequent games featured a more restrained set-up by White with 13 f3, a good example being J.Smejkal-A.Yusupov, German League 1992, which went 13...Kh8 14 b3 Ng8 15 exf5 (White usually plays this when Black can't recapture with the knight) 15...Bxf5 16 d4 Bh3 17 Ndc3 Bxg2 18 Kxg2 exd4 19 Nxd4 Nge7 20 Bg1 Nxd4 21 Bxd4 Nf5 22 Bxg7+ Nxg7 and Black gradually equalized. There's no doubt that this is a serious line for White and Yusupov's defence represents a good model.

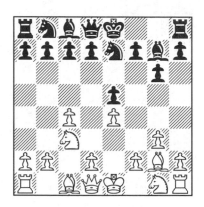

Diagram 11 (B)

Botvinnik vs the Botvinnik!

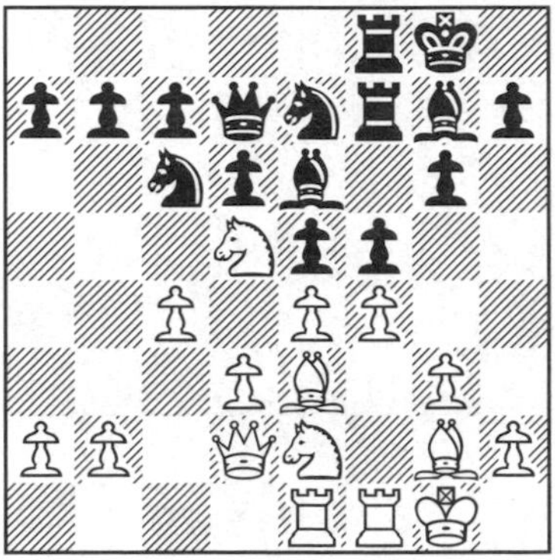

Diagram 12 (B)

This break leaves e4 weak

13...fxe4 14 dxe4 Nc8!

Getting ready to exchange the light-squared bishops with ...Be6-h3, as the rook on f7 would defend c7. Once these bishops have been exchanged the e4-pawn can become tender.

15 c5

In later games White preferred 15 b3 at this point, for example 15...Bh3 16 Rf2 Bxg2 17 Kxg2 exf4 18 gxf4 Re8 19 Qd3 Qg4+ 20 Ng3 Nb6 brought about a double-edged struggle in W.Schmidt-V.Jansa, Polanica Zdroj 1969.

15...Bh3 16 b4 Bxg2 17 Kxg2 exf4 18 gxf4 Re8 19 Ng3

Botvinnik suggested that 19 Nec3 might have been stronger. Benko is naturally keen on bringing a knight over to defend his king, but Black's next move proves to be unpleasant.

19...h5! (Diagram 13) 20 b5

The immediate 20 f5 fails after 20...h4 21 fxg6 Rxf1 22 Rxf1 (or 22 Nxf1 Rxe4) 22...hxg3 23 Rf7 Qg4 24 Rxg7+ Kxg7 25 Bh6+ Kxg6 and White's attack runs out of steam. Botvinnik also pointed out that 20 h4 is met by 20...Qg4, though this is less clear after 21 b5 Nd8 22 Qd1.

20...N6e7 21 f5!?

If now 21 h4, there follows 21...Nxd5 22 Qxd5 Qxb5.

21...h4 22 fxg6

Black can answer 22 f6 with 22...Nxd5 23 Qxd5 Re5.

22...Rxf1 23 Rxf1 hxg3 24 Rf7

24 Bh6? is refuted by 24...Qg4 25 Bxg7 Qxe4+ 26 Kh3 Qe6+ 27 Kxg3 Qxg6+ etc.

24...Be5! (Diagram 14)

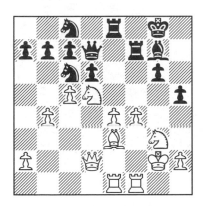

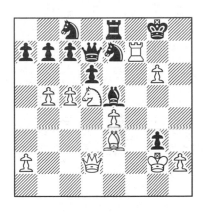

Diagram 13 (W)

Initiating kingside action

Diagram 14 (W)

A key defensive move

After 24...Qg4? White's attack comes crashing through with 25 Rxg7+! Kxg7 26 Qd4+ Kxg6 27 Qf6+ Kh7 28 Qf7+ Qg7 29 Nf6+ Kh8 30 Qh5+ and mate next move.

25 Bd4

Black can meet 25 Qe2 with 25...Qe6 and then taking the pawn on g6.

25...Qg4 26 Rf4?

A mistake in time trouble, which makes it easy for Black.

The critical line was 26 Bxe5, but after 26...gxh2+ 27 Bg3 Qxe4+ 28 Kxh2 Qxg6 (not 28...Qxd5?? 29 Qh6 and wins) 29 Nxe7+ Rxe7 30 Rxe7 Nxe7 31 cxd6 Nf5 32 Qd5+ Kf8 33 Qf3 (if 33 dxc7? Qxg3+ 34 Kh1 Qe1+ 35 Kh2 Qf2+ 36 Qg2 Qf4+ and ...Qxc7, or 35 Kg2 Ne3+ 36 Kf3 Nxd5 37 c8Q+ Qe8 would win in the end) 33...cxd6 34 Bf2 White still faces a difficult endgame.

26...Qh5

Threatening both ...Qxh2+ and ...Nxd5.

27 Bxe5 Qxh2+ 28 Kf3 Qxd2 29 Nf6+ Kg7 30 Nxe8+ Kxg6 31 Rf6+ Kh7 32 Bxg3 Qd3+ 33 Kf2 Qxb5 34 cxd6 Qxe8 0-1

1 c4 g6 2 Nc3 Bg7 3 g3 e5 4 Bg2 d6 5 e3 Nc6 6 Nge2 h5 (Diagram 15)

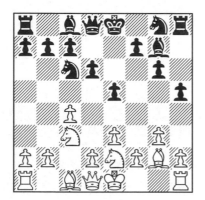

Diagram 15 (W)	**Diagram 16 (W)**
An aggressive response	Vacating e5 for the knight

7 h4

White has also tried ignoring the h-pawn with 7 d4, though Black certainly has counterplay after 7...h4 8 d5 Nce7 9 e4 f5. K.Hulak-Z.Almasi, Pula 2001, continued 10 Bg5 h3 11 Bf3 Nf6 12 0-0 0-0 13 Qd2 Nh7 14 Be3 f4! 15 gxf4 exf4 16 Bd4 Bh6 17 c5 Ng5 18 Bh1 Nf7 19 cxd6 cxd6 and Black had gained control of the vital e5-square.

7...Bg4! 8 d3

R.Etruk-L.Stein, Tallinn 1969, varied here with 8 Qa4, but then 8...Nge7 9 b4 a6 10 Bb2 0-0 11 Qb3 Be6 12 a4 a5! 13 b5 Nb4 14 Nd5 Nexd5 15 cxd5 Bg4 left Black with the better game.

8...Nge7 9 b4! a6!

Holding up White's plan of b4-b5. If 9...Nxb4 10 Rb1 would recover the pawn with advantage.

10 Rb1 Rb8 11 Qc2

Now Black was ready to meet 11 a4 with 11...a5! 12 b5 Nb4 as in the Stein game above; while after 13 Ba3 he could defend the knight with 13...c5.

11...0-0 12 Bd2 Qd7 13 Nd5! b5! 14 a4

On 14 Nec3 bxc4 15 dxc4 Black can play a similar pawn sac to the game with 15...e4!, clearing e5 for his knight.

14...e4! (Diagram 16) 15 Nxe7+

After both 15 Bxe4 Ne5! and 15 dxe4?! bxc4 16 Qxc4 Nxd5 17 Qxd5 Ne5 we see Black's knight leap into the middle with powerful effect.

15...Qxe7 16 Bxe4?!

16 d4! was better, in order to prevent ...Ne5. Nunn then gave the variation 16...Bf3 17 Bxf3 exf3 18 cxb5 Na7! 19 Ng1! axb5 20 Nxf3 bxa4 21 Qxa4 Qe4 22 Qd1, but Black has just 22...Bxd4 at the end of this.

16...Ne5

Threatening 17...bxc4 18 dxc4 Nf3+ 19 Kf1 Qxe4! 20 Qxd5 Nxd2+ etc.

17 cxb5 axb5 18 axb5 d5! 19 Bg2

On 19 Bxd5 there would follow 19...Rfd8 20 Be4 (or 20 Bc4 Bf5 21 Nf4 Bh6 22 0-0 Bxf4 23 exf4 Nxc4 24 Qxc4 Bxd3) 20...Nf3+! 21 Bxf3 Bxf3 22 Rg1 Rxb5 with a powerful initiative for the sacrificed pawns.

19...Nf3+ 20 Kf1 Rxb5 21 Ng1 Nxd2+ 22 Qxd2 Rfb8 23 d4 c5! (Diagram 17)

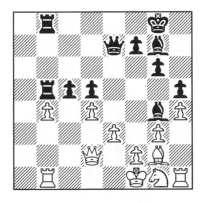

Diagram 17 (W)

Smashing the position open

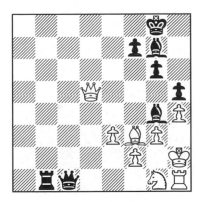

Diagram 18 (B)

The losing move

Smashing the position open to exploit the vulnerability of the white king. This is stronger than 23...Bf5 24 Rb3 Rxb4 25 Rxb4 Rxb4 26 Bxd5 Rb1+ 27 Kg2 Be4+ 28 Bxe4 Qxe4+ 29 Kh2 followed by Qe2, when White survives.

24 dxc5 Qxc5 25 Bf3

25 bxc5?? goes down immediately to 25...Rxb1+ 26 Qe1 Rxe1+ 27 Kxe1 Bc3+ 28 Kf1 Rb1 mate.

25...Rxb4 26 Rxb4 Rxb4 27 Qxd5 Rb1+ 28 Kg2 Qc1 29 Kh2? (Diagram 18)

Losing. White should have played 29 Qd3 to cover the f1-square.

29...Qf1 30 Bg2 Qxf2 31 Nh3?

31 Qe4 would have been more tenacious, but Black is still winning after 31...Bf6!
32 Qf4 Qxf4 33 exf4 Rb2.

31...Rxh1+ 32 Kxh1 Bxh3 33 Bxh3 Qxg3 0-1

Game 57
☐ **M.Berkovich** ■ **N.Davies**
Tel Aviv 1992

---

1 c4 g6 2 Nc3 Bg7 3 g3 Nc6 4 Bg2 d6 5 Nf3 e5 6 d3 f5 7 0-0 Nf6 8 Nd5

Rather than play for b2-b4 White invites Black to take on d5 and open the c-file. In
theory this looks like a good plan, but I don't think it causes Black too many problems in practice.

8...0-0 9 Bg5 Ne7 10 Nxf6+ Bxf6 11 Bxf6 Rxf6 12 c5 Nc6 (Diagram 19)

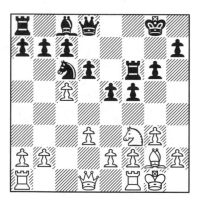

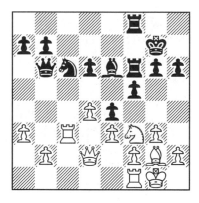

Diagram 19 (W)	Diagram 20 (W)
Black has no real problems	Securing a space advantage

13 cxd6

The game S.Vijayalakshmi-D.Howell, Torquay 2002, varied at this point with 13
Qb3+ Kg7 14 cxd6 cxd6 15 Rfc1, which should probably have been met by 15...Qe7
intending 16...Be6, rather than 15...d5?! 16 Rc5 when White had some pressure in
the game.

13...cxd6 14 Rc1 Kg7 15 e3 Qb6 16 Qd2 Be6 17 a3 h6 18 Rc3 Raf8 19 d4 e4 (Diagram 20)

Securing a nice space advantage. White's bishop on g2 in particular is inhibited by the pawn on e4.

20 Ne1 Ne7 21 f3 Bd5 22 fxe4 Bxe4 23 Bxe4 fxe4 24 Rxf6 Rxf6 25 Qe2 Nd5 26 Rc1 Qb3 27 Ng2 b5 (Diagram 21)

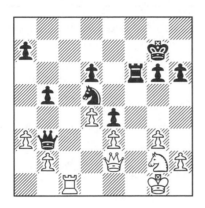

Diagram 21 (W)

The queenside pawns advance

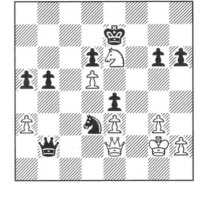

Diagram 22 (W)

Queens off for an easy win

28 Rf1 Rxf1+ 29 Kxf1 a5

Should Black win the b2-pawn he'll want his own queenside pawns as near to the queening squares as possible.

30 Kf2 Nb6

Honing in on the weaknesses at b2 and e3.

31 Nf4 Nc4 32 Ne6+?

32 Nxg6!? is an interesting try which gives perpetual check if the knight is taken. But it looks as if the knight endgame arising from 32...Qxb2 33 Qxb2 Nxb2 is winning for Black, for example 34 Ne7 Nc4 35 g4 b4 36 axb4 axb4 37 Nf5+ Kf6 38 Ng3 d5 39 h4 b3 40 Ne2 b2 41 Nc3 Kg6 42 Nb1 h5 43 g5 Nd6 44 Kg3 Nf5+ winning either e3 or h4.

32...Kf6 33 Nc7

After 33 Nf4 Nxb2 34 Qg4 Black gets a winning queen endgame via 34...Nd3+ 35 Nxd3 Qc2+ 36 Ke1 Qc3+ 37 Kf2 Qd2+ 38 Kg1 Qxd3, only capturing on d3 after driving the white king to a bad square. Should White then play 39 Qh4+, Black's king heads for the queenside with 39...Ke6 40 Qxh6 Kd5.

33...Nxb2 34 Kg2 Nd3 35 d5 Ke7 36 Ne6 Qb2 (Diagram 22)

The simplest way to avoid any danger of a perpetual

37 Qxb2 Nxb2 38 Nd4 Nc4 39 Kf2 Nxa3 40 Nc6+ Kf6 41 Nxa5 Ke5 0-1

Game 58
□ **L.Psakhis** ■ **G.Kasparov**
La Manga (5th matchgame) 1990

1 c4 g6 2 Nc3 Bg7 3 g3 Nc6 4 Bg2 d6 5 Nf3 e5 6 d3 f5 7 0-0 Nf6 8 Rb1 h6! (Diagram 23)

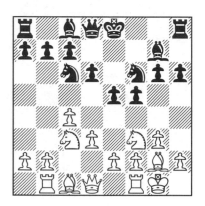

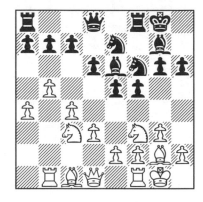

Diagram 23 (W)   **Diagram 24 (W)**

A useful little move   An instructive finesse

Both preventing Bc1-g5 and preparing a kingside pawn advance.

9 b4 0-0

NOTE: While castling is often a good move, don't do so automatically in the Modern. For example, there's a good alternative in 9...g5 here.

10 b5 Ne7 11 a4 Be6! (Diagram 24) 12 Ba3

I must say that the precision of Kasparov's opening play is very impressive here. The point of his 11...Be6 finesse (rather than the immediate 11...g5) is that 12 c5? dxc5 13 Nxe5 Ne8! skewers White's knights on e5 and c3, while 14 f4 is answered by 14...Qd4+. Another point is that 12 Nd2 can be met by 12...d5, so White has little choice apart from 12 Ba3 if he wants to pursue his queenside ambitions.

12...Rc8!

Preparing to secure his queenside with 13...b6. As noted in the introduction, the immediate 12...b6? runs into 13 Nxe5! and if 13...dxe5 14 Bxa8 Qxa8 15 Bxe7 etc.

13 Nd2

Possibly White should have tried 13 c5, after which 13...b6 14 cxd6 cxd6 15 Qd2

Qd7 16 Rfc1 g5 17 Na2! followed by 18 Nb4 would take aim at the c6-square.

13...b6 14 e3

Preparing central action to counter Black's kingside storm. Otherwise 14 a5 g5 15 axb6 axb6 16 Bb2 Qd7 17 Ra1 was possible, but not particularly pleasant for White.

14...g5 15 d4 exd4 16 exd4 f4!? (Diagram 25)

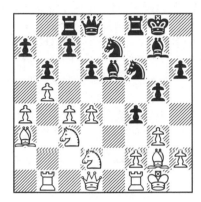

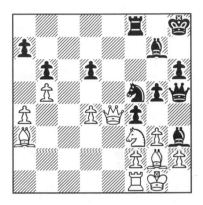

Diagram 25 (W)	Diagram 26 (W)
Black starts the attack	Beginning a mating attack

17 Re1

For a while White defends with great skill. The dangers of Black's attack are seen after 17 gxf4 Ng6! 18 fxg5 Ng4! (Psakhis), for example 19 gxh6 Qh4 20 h3 Rxf2! 21 hxg4 Bxd4, or 19 Ne2 Nh4, or 19 h3 Nxf2! 20 Rxf2 Rxf2 21 Kxf2 Bxd4+ etc.

17...Bg4 18 Nf3! Qd7 19 c5 Rce8 20 Rc1! Nf5 21 Qd3 Kh8!

21...dxc5?! 22 Qc4+ Kh8 23 dxc5 gives White counterplay.

22 cxd6?!

22 Qc4 was better here; and White's next move only encourages the black queen to go to h5.

22...cxd6 23 Rxe8?! Qxe8! 24 Rf1 Qh5 25 Ne4

25 Ne5! was a better try, playing for complications.

25...Nxe4 26 Qxe4 Bh3 (Diagram 26)

Threatening to start a mating attack with 26...Bxg2 27 Kxg2 g4, followed by ...f4-f3+ and ...Qh3 etc.

27 Ne5?!

With the idea that 27...dxe5? 28 Bxf8 Bxf8 29 Qxe5+ starts a vicious counterattack, but Black can decline the offer.

27...Bxg2! 28 Kxg2 g4 29 Bxd6 Rf6

29...fxg3! 30 hxg3 Qh3+ 31 Kg1 Qxf1+! 32 Kxf1 Nxg3+ was also good.

30 Bb8 Qh3+ 31 Kg1 f3 32 Nxf3 gxf3 33 Qxf3 Nh4 0-1

Summary

1...g6 is an excellent response to both 1 c4 and 1 Nf3, especially if White insists on his favourite English or Réti formation. The point is that Black can often play 2...Bg7 and 3...e5 without committing any of his other pawns or pieces. He is thus able to adapt to whichever set-up White then adopts, a strategy which is very much in keeping with the Modern spirit.

Test Positions

It is Black to play in all positions.

1. J.Arnason-R.Keene

London Lloyds Bank 1981

3. S.Leiser-N.Davies

Hamburg 1995

2. L.Ljubojevic-J.Timman

Malaga 1971

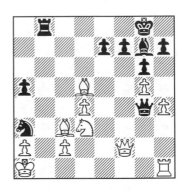

4. L.Yudasin-E.Gufeld

USSR 1985

5. Y.Afek-N.Davies
Herzliya 1993

8. G.Sigurjonsson-J.Timman
Wijk aan Zee 1980

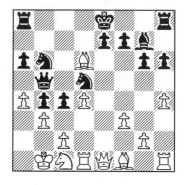

6. H.Spangenberg-Z.Azmaiparashvili
Moscow Olympiad 1994

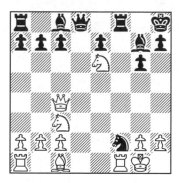

9. F.Roeder-O.Reeh
German League 1985

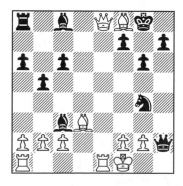

7. L.Day-O.Jackson
New Zealand Ch'ship, Wellington 1974

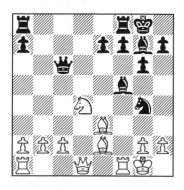

10. D.Belfiore-M.Ginsburg
Acasusso 1991

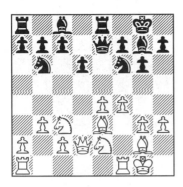

11. J.Shaw-C.McNab
Scottish Ch'ship, St Andrews 1993

14. A.Medina Garcia-B.Larsen
Las Palmas 1972

12. I.Ostry-W.Hook
Moscow Olympiad 1994

15. R.Watanabe-D.Norwood
World Junior Ch'ship, Adelaide 1988

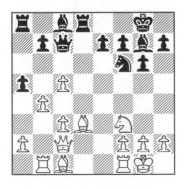

13. J.Lechtynsky-A.Kubicek
Czechoslovakian Ch'ship, Trinec 1972

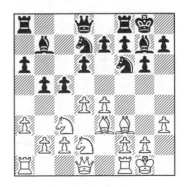

16. R.Balasubramaniun-D.Norwood
Calcutta 1994

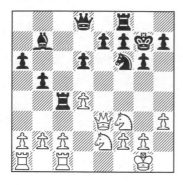

17. M.Thesing-A.Miles
Bad Wörishofen 1989

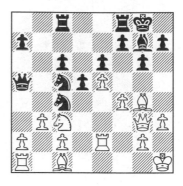

20. Y.Giorgadze-Ma.Tseitlin
USSR Team Championship 1975

18. G.Kamsky-Z.Azmaiparashvili
Brussels (rapid) 1992

21. M.Dutreeuw-J.Speelman
Antwerp 1993

19. M.Palac-I.Lechtynsky
Rimavska Sobota 1990

22. V.Korchnoi-Z.Azmaiparashvili
Amsterdam 1990

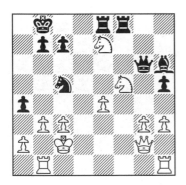

23. G.Waddingham-N.Davies
British Championship, Southport 1983

26. A.Breedveld-M.Bosboom
Enschede 1992

24. S.Guliev-A.Kakageldyev
Simferopol 1989

27. N.Kalesis-E.Grivas
Corfu 1991

25. P.Littlewood-N.Davies
ARC Young Masters, Westergate 1987

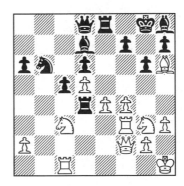

28. V.Bagirov-J.Bednarski
Polanica Zdroj 1969

29. B.Wagner-E.Prie
Strasbourg 1991

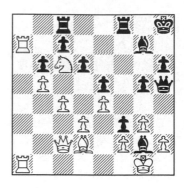

30. I.Johannsson-A.J.Mestel
Lucerne Olympiad 1982

Solutions

1) 31...Qxc4!! 32 Bxc4 Bxc3+ 33 Qb2 Bxe1! 34 Bxe2 Bg3! 0-1. White cannot meet the threat of 35...Be5.

2) 21...Rd2! (threatening the bishop on e2) **22 g3** (22 Nxd2 is answered by 22...Nh3+ 23 gxh3 Qxh2 mate; 22 Nbd4 is a better try, when Black could play 22...Bd5 23 g3 Nh3+ 24 Kh1 Ng5 25 Ne6+ Nxe6 26 Qxg4 Rxb2, but this isn't as easy as the game) **22...Nxe2+ 23 Rxe2 Rxe2 24 Nbd4 Nxh2 0-1**.

3) 21...Rxd2! 0-1. After 22 Nxd2 Nd4 White is defenceless against the threat of ...Qxc2 mate.

4) 33...Bxd4! 34 Bxf7+ Kf8 35 Qd2 (if 35 Bxd4 Qxd4+ 36 Qxd4 Nxc2 mate) **35...Bxc3+** (35...Qe2 or 35...Qg2 would also win; but not 35...Kxf7? 36 Ne5+ Bxe5 37 Bxe5 which resulted in a draw in the game) **36 Qxc3 Qd4!** and if **37 Qxd4 Nxc2** is mate again.

5) 10...Qg4! 11 Kf1 (or 11 Nxe5 Qxg2 12 Qf3 Qxg5) **11...Nxf3 12 Bxf6 Nxh2+ 13 Rxh2 Qxd1+ 14 Nxd1 Bxf6** and Black was a good pawn up.

6) 18...Nxa4! 19 bxa4 Qxa4 20 Bxc4 (after 20 Ne2 one way to win is with 20...b3 21 cxb3 Qxb3+ 22 Kc1 Ne3 23 Qd2 Qxd1+ etc) **20...Nc3+ 21 Qxc3 bxc3 22 Bb3 Qa5** and White had inadequate compensation for the queen.

7) Black saved a draw with **17...Ne3+! 18 fxe3** (18 Rxe3? Qh1+ 19 Ke2 Bg4+ wins for Black) **18...Qh1+ 19 Kf2 Bxe1+ 20 Rxe1 Qh4+ 21 Kf1 Qh1+ 22 Kf2 Qh4+ 23 Kf1 Qh1+ ½-½**.

8) 23...Rxb2! 24 Kxb2 Qb7+ 25 Kc1 f5! 0-1. White's queen must vacate the d1-h5 diagonal, whereupon 26...Ne2+! 27 Nxe2 Qb2 mates.

9) 14...Nh3+ 15 gxh3 Rxf1+ 16 Kxf1 Qg8! recovered the piece with advantage, and Black went on to win.

10) 18...Qxg2+! 19 Kxg2 Nxe3+ 20 Kg1 Nxd1 won a pawn and subsequently the game.

11) 13...Bxh3! 14 Bxh3 Nxe4 15 Nxe4 Qxe4 16 Kf2?? (16 Bxb6 axb6 17 Rae1 Rxa2 18 Nc3 Qd4+ 19 Qxd4+ Bxd4 20 Kh1 Rxe1 21 Nxa2 Re2 would probably end in a draw) **16...Nd5 17 Bd4 Qxe2+! 18 Qxe2 Bxd4+ 19 Kf3 Rxe2 20 Kxe2 Re8+ 0-1**. Black has recovered the piece with two pawns interest.

12) 8...Bf3! won the exchange, which Black consolidated after **9 fxe5 Bxh1 10 exd6 Qxd6 11 Bb5+ Kf8 12 Qxd6+ cxd6 13 Nge2 Bf3 14 h3 Be5 15 Nd4 Bg2 16 0-0-0 Bxh3** and went on to win.

13) 15...Rxd3! 16 Qxd3 Bf5 won material.

14) 21...c5! 22 Nxc5 Qxc5 23 Re8+ Rf8 24 Bxc5 Rxd2 25 Bxf8 Bxf8 brought about a position in which Black's two bishops were stronger than the rook and two pawns.

15) 14...Bxe5! 15 Bxe5 Qg5 16 g4 Qxe5 17 gxh5 gxh5 threatening 18...Qg5+, or 18...Kh8 followed by 19...Rg8+. The best White could find was **18 f4 Qc5+ 19 Kh2 Qxc4 20 Qxh5** when he was a pawn down for nothing.

16) 11...Ng4! 12 Bxg4 cxd4 13 Bxd4 Bxd4 gave Black the advantage because of his powerful dark-squared bishop.

17) 18...Qa8! threatened to double White's pawns with ...Bxf3, which he should probably have prevented with 19 Ne1. Instead the game continued **19 c3?! Bxf3 20 Qxf3 Qxf3 21 gxf3 Rc7 22 Kf1 Rb8** and Black eventually ground out the victory.

18) 15...Nde5! 16 dxe5 Nxe5 17 Qb5 Nxf3+ 18 Kg2 Ne5 gave Black a clear advantage, though this didn't stop White winning in the end!

19) 20...Nh4! 21 gxh4? (but if 21 f4 Qg4 22 Qd1 Rxf4! wins a pawn for nothing) **21...Rxf3 22 Qd1** (Black is also winning after 22 Qc2 Qg4+ 23 Ng3 Nf4 24 Qd1 Ne2+ 25 Qxe2 Rxg3+, or 22 Qxf3 Rxf3 23 Rxf3 Qg4+ 24 Bg3 Qxe4) **22...Qg4+ 23 Ng3 Nxg3 24 hxg3** (24 Bxg3 Rxf1+ wins the queen) **24...Rxf2 0-1**, because 25 Qxg4 Rxf1+ 26 Kg2 R8f2+ 27 Kh3 Rh1 is mate.

20) 21...Nd6! 22 Qe1 Nde4 brought Black's knight to a dominating square and gave him the advantage after **23 Nxe4 Qxe1+ 24 Rxe1 Nxe4 25 Bf3 f5**.

21) 26...Bxg4! won a pawn and ruined White's kingside, since if 27 hxg4 Qxg4+ regains the piece on f3.

22) 10...Nxd4! won a pawn for nothing, as 11 cxd4? Bxd4 would net a second one (as White must play 12 Nc3 to save the rook in the corner).

23) 39...Rxe7! 40 Nxe7 Rf2+! 41 Qxf2 Qxe4+ 42 Kd1 (if 42 Kb2 Nd3+ wins the queen) **42...Qxb1+ 43 Ke2 Qe4+** picked up the h1-rook with check as well.

24) 31...Nxd5! 32 exd5 Rf4 0-1, as White has no good answer to the threat of 33...Rh5 trapping his queen.

25) 47...Qh4! 48 Bg4 (if 48 Qxh4 Rg1 mate) **48...Rxg4 49 Qxd4+ Nf6 50 b5 Rg3 51 Rxg3 Bxg3** left White defenceless.

26) 27...Nh6! is a far from obvious move, but leaves White with no good defence to 28...f5. White played **28 Rd3**, but resigned before Black replied with the devastating 28...Rxe4!.

27) 27...Bxb2! won a pawn for starters, the game finishing **28 Bg5 Qf2 29 Qb1** (if 29 Be3 Qxe2!) **29...Re8 30 Qd1 Bc3 31 Bd2 Bxd2 32 Qxd2 Bd5 0-1**, due to decisive threat of 33...Bc4.

28) 24...Bg4! 25 Bg5 (25 hxg4 Qh4+ 26 Kg1 Qxh6 leaves White weak on the dark squares, though this was probably better than the game) **25...f6 26 hxg4** (26 Bxf6 Qxf6 27 hxg4 Qh4+ 28 Kg1 Rc4 has the unpleasant threat of 29...Bd4] **26...fxg5 27 f5 Nd7** and Black's dark square control, in particular of the e5-square, gave him a clear advantage.

29) 24...Rxf3! won immediately, since if 25 Qxf3 Qxe1+ or 25 Rxf3 Bg2 mate.

30) 28...Bf1! was good for Black, though White's resignation was somewhat premature. After 29 Qb1! (not 29 Rxf1? Qh3 or 29 Kxf1? Qxh2 and mates) 29...Be2 30 Kh1 Qh3 31 Qg1 Bxd3 32 Ne7! g4 33 Nxc8 Rxc8 Black has more than enough for the exchange, but still needs to win.

Index of Complete Games

Index of Variations

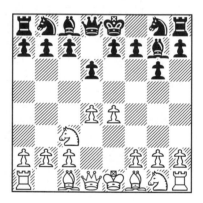

...Bg7

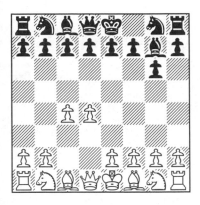

1 c4

1...g6 2 Nc3 Bg7

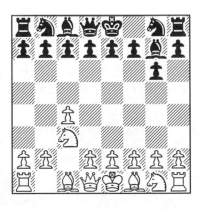